PRAISE FOR

THE FORGOTTEN GOSPEL

I never thought I'd see the day a book like this is written and published, and am delighted to be proven wrong. With thoughtfulness and humility, Brianna invites us to wade into the self-disclosed revelation of the holy Word... *The Forgotten Gospel* illuminates the foundations of the covenantal commonwealth and is a worthy read for all Gentiles grateful to be grafted into its promises. I pray it ignites new wonder in the Body of Jesus.

STEPHANIE QUICK | THE EMMAUS TABLE

In *The Forgotten Gospel* Brianna Tittel has given us a personal and accessible entry point into the difficult issues that arise when thoughtful Christians read the entire Bible... You will find yourself pondering questions you didn't know existed and discover new depth and beauty in the story of Jesus as the Messiah of Israel. If you're looking for an honest and thorough account of how to read the Bible as a coherent whole centered on Jesus, you'll find it here.

TIM MACKIE | CO-FOUNDER, BIBLEPROJECT

As Jewish followers of Jesus who spend our lives helping the church reconnect with its biblical roots, we recognize how easily the gospel becomes detached from its original context. This book does the important work of restoring that connection and recovering what was always there. In *The Forgotten Gospel*, Brianna illustrates the importance of an unbroken Jewish storyline that finds its fulfillment in Jesus. Brianna allows Leviticus to speak as Scripture, as covenant, and as the framework Jesus himself lived within, and invites readers into a faith that is historically rooted, biblically faithful, and spiritually alive.

RON & MATT DAVIS | FOUNDERS, THE JEWISH ROAD

As a Jewish believer in Yeshua, I read the Scriptures from within the tradition they were written to. When I opened *The Forgotten Gospel*, I expected the usual Christian attempt to explain Leviticus through a lens that ultimately dismisses it. What I found instead was something I rarely encounter: a Gentile believer who has done the hard, honest work of letting the text speak on its own terms. She says all of this not from a Messianic Jewish pulpit, but from within the very Evangelical world that most needs to hear it.

This book is not asking you to become Jewish. It is asking you to stop ignoring the Jewishness of the Messiah you claim to follow. Read this book slowly. Let it challenge what you think you know. And when you feel the ground shifting beneath your assumptions, do not retreat. Press in. That is where the real encounter begins.

SERGIO DESOTO | AUTHOR AND JOURNALIST

As a lifelong apprentice of Messiah Jesus and the Hebrew Scriptures, I thank God for Tittel's book—a true gift to the church! *The Forgotten Gospel* delivers top-shelf biblical scholarship in a manner accessible to even the newest follower of Jesus. Tittel convincingly shows that when Jesus claimed to fulfill the Law and the Prophets he wasn't setting them aside… If you want to cultivate a life shaped by every book of the Bible—including Leviticus—*The Forgotten Gospel* is the perfect place to start.

PAUL GODBOUT | ASSOCIATE PASTOR,
CAPITAL CHURCH, SALT LAKE CITY

A refreshing and well-written invitation to reconsider the importance of one of the most neglected books of Scripture…I applaud Tittel's commitment to encouraging Christians to wrestle more deeply and carefully with the whole of Scripture.

DAVID WILBER | AUTHOR, *BORN AGAIN TO A LIVING HOPE*

THE FORGOTTEN GOSPEL

REIMAGINING LEVITICUS *and the* STORY OF JESUS

BRIANNA TITTEL

THE FORGOTTEN GOSPEL

Copyright © 2026 by Brianna Tittel

All rights reserved.

Published by Two Stones Press.

For more information, visit briannatittel.com.

This book reflects the author's research and theological interpretation of Scripture. It is not intended to replace personal study, communal discernment, or pastoral counsel.

Book designed by Mark Karis.

First edition

ISBN: [Paperback ISBN]: 979-8-9951745-3-0
ISBN: [eBook ISBN]: 979-8-9951745-6-1

Printed in the United States of America

CONTENTS

INTRODUCTION

WHY THIS BOOK?

I never set out to write a book about Leviticus, or to write a book at all. I'm just a normal person like anyone else: a mom of four, a former high school teacher, and someone who loves asking questions and exploring the story of the Bible. Somehow that curiosity led me to wrestle with one of the hardest books in Scripture—and then to write about what I found.

Why? Because I believe that ordinary people should be able to open their Bibles and make sense of the hard parts. Scripture should stir our questions, challenge our assumptions, and draw us closer to God. Reading it should excite, compel, and change us.

But that was not my experience with Leviticus. I had read it once or twice. I knew what it said. I knew, in theory, that Jesus "fulfilled" everything in it. What more could there really be in all those outmoded laws? So I did what most of us do with Leviticus: I ignored it.

When we don't understand the hard parts of Scripture, this is what usually happens. We push them aside and get comfortable leaving them untouched. We come up with ways to reassure ourselves that skipping them doesn't really matter. That's exactly what I did for most of my life. Leviticus sat on the sidelines, and I didn't look back.

But Jesus didn't sideline Leviticus. Neither did the apostles. They lived it out. The book I read once and flipped right past was life-giving to them. So I began to wonder, why wasn't it life-giving to me or any other Christian I knew? Why did it feel so out of touch with anything I could actually live by?

When I brought this question up with pastors I trusted, their answers were always gracious, but unhelpful. They'd praise my efforts to learn, direct me to a commentary or two, and then say something like: *Leviticus was for Israel back then. It gives context to the rest of the Bible, but we don't need its practices anymore. You just need to understand the cultural rituals and then you'll see how Jesus has fulfilled it for us today. Just focus on loving Jesus.* But these answers didn't satisfy me. If Jesus fulfilled Leviticus, why didn't it feel full and rich when I read it? If I had asked the same question about the Gospel of John or the Psalms, no one would have tossed me a commentary and told me to simply move on.

That question of whether Leviticus mattered gnawed at me, especially because Jesus himself seemed to say something very different. In the Sermon on the Mount, he declared: "Do not think that I have come to abolish the Law or the Prophets. I have not come to abolish them, but to fulfill them. ... not an iota, not a dot, will pass from the Law until all is accomplished" (Matthew 5:17–18). Jesus warned that he didn't come to abolish Leviticus. He placed the law front and center. Everyone within Christianity affirms Jesus's words. But in practice, it appears that we all believe Leviticus is *fulfilled* because Jesus *replaced* all that it entails.

While scholars have certainly written on its contents, within the Evangelical movement Leviticus is treated as though Jesus stepped into its story, completed everything it commands, and—poof—box checked, move on. Even with the best intentions, theologians from Augustine and Aquinas to Luther and Calvin have approached it this way. Leviticus is often seen as something we've outgrown—either replaced through fulfillment in Christ and transformed by new forms of worship, or divided into categories of relevant and irrelevant law, with only the moral principles retained for Christians to keep. That attitude has trickled down to the rest of us, leaving the impression that we have no further responsibility to the book. But that's not what Jesus said. So the question driving this book was born: *Did Jesus actually replace Leviticus at the cross?* My answer is simple but disruptive: he didn't.

This is a book about the cost of leaving Leviticus out of the story— and how neglecting it blinds us to who Jesus really is, undermines what he came to accomplish, and obscures the good news that Leviticus itself proclaims. Leviticus remains essential to understanding God's plan and Jesus's mission. When we restore it to its rightful place and let it shape how we read the rest of Scripture, we begin to see that everything it describes was meant to continue alongside our risen Lord.

MY APPROACH—AN HONEST OVERVIEW

The perspective you'll find in this book is probably different from what you've heard in mainstream Christianity. I mean no disrespect to pastors, teachers, or scholars—they've done remarkable work, much of which I've relied on. But as I wrestled with my own questions about Leviticus, the answers I often found didn't satisfy me. I wondered what we were missing by leaving it out of the conversation. The assumptions I challenge here are ones I once shared myself—deeply rooted in Evangelical teaching and inherited through centuries of Christian interpretation.

The problem, I realized, is how we usually read books like Leviticus. When Christians study the Old Testament, we often read Jesus *back* into it. Because Leviticus feels foreign, we use the New Testament as a shortcut: "Jesus is my Great High Priest, the atoning sacrifice—Hebrews explains everything." But that's a backward hermeneutic. It forces the meaning of earlier texts to be determined by later ones. Jesus didn't read himself into Leviticus; he let Leviticus define him. The Old Testament gave him the framework for understanding who he was and what he came to do.

This book approaches Scripture in the same way, through three complementary lenses: *holistic, messianic, and post-supersessionist.*

HOLISTIC, because I believe the Bible (in the Protestant canon) is a continuous, unified story whose earliest pages still inform its end.

MESSIANIC, because I believe the whole story is about God's work in the world being accomplished through Israel's Messiah, Jesus of Nazareth—the one who fulfills and completes God's purposes in perfect continuity.

POST-SUPERSESSIONIST, because I'm reading the Bible—and in particular the New Testament—as a set of Jewish documents, part of an ongoing, internal Jewish conversation. Put simply, *supersessionism* claims that the church replaces Israel and generally holds the Old Testament should be understood mainly through later Christian interpretations. A post-supersessionist reading pushes against that instinct, resisting the urge to read later Christian understandings back into texts that did not arise from a Christian worldview. It invites us to step into the world of Judaism and let *that* worldview—the one in which these texts were actually written—carry us forward, something most Christians have little experience with.

These, I believe, are the lenses that Jesus and the biblical authors used, and the paradigm by which the Bible seems to interpret its own story. Underlying these convictions is a simple one: the Bible should be read in a reasonably straightforward way—a natural reading that honors the text within its own literary, historical, and situational context. When we let the words speak in their own world first, their meaning becomes far more coherent and compelling within the bigger, unified story that they're a part of. Most believers would agree with this in theory, yet in practice our reading habits often drift in a different direction. Christian tradition has tended to interpret the Old Testament through the lens of the New, rather than through the eyes of its original authors. This has led to the belief that books like Leviticus require new revelation in Christ and the Holy Spirit to be rightly understood or faithfully applied.

But the Spirit of God has always been present with his people, illuminating truth through meditation and obedience. Later writings and events deepen our understanding, but they do not revise what came before. The same God who spoke through Moses still speaks through his Word today, unchanged in his character and consistent in his purposes. Our task is not to improve upon original revelation, but to listen more carefully to it within the context of our own lives.

For that reason, I embrace a reading of Scripture that seeks to hear the entire Bible through the voice of the God of Abraham, his Messiah, and the worldview of its authors. The New Testament writings were never meant to be severed from the world of first-century Judaism or the people who lived by it. The apostles' letters were not the founding documents of a new religion but testimonies to God's covenant faithfulness within Israel's story—now unfolding among the nations after Jesus's ascension.

As time went on, however, the relationship between the Gentile and Jewish followers of Jesus grew strained. Gentile believers, who entered the faith during periods of intense Roman persecution against the Jews, had compelling reasons to distance themselves from Jewish identity. Over time, that separation hardened into suspicion, then theology, and finally tradition. Much of the church's later self-understanding—and even the formation of the New Testament canon—emerged within a cultural climate marked by growing anti-Jewish sentiment, fueled by both political tensions and social pressures of survival under Roman rule. Early church theologians and bishops were not all malicious in their intent, and many traditions todays hold a deep reverence for the earliest books of the Bible. But we'd be lying to ourselves if we didn't acknowledge that their efforts to define Christianity as distinct from Judaism did leave deep interpretive scars and, often, a low view of the Old Testament, its people, and its story.

My goal is not to condemn them or discredit their work, but to return to a moment before those divisions calcified—to hear Scripture as it might have sounded in the first century. I recognize that this differs from Catholic, Orthodox, and certain Protestant traditions, which honor the early church's liturgical and cultural inheritance alongside Scripture itself. Those traditions have preserved many treasures. But my conviction is that Scripture remains coherent and authoritative on its own terms, and that situating it within its native context can help all believers see the gospel's continuity and depth more clearly. I'm not suggesting that every reader should reconstruct theology based on their own personal conclusions by reading only through the eyes of the original writers. Rather, I'm advocating for a sympathetic reading—one that honors our ancient neighbors through whom these texts were given, and acknowledges that our theology ought to grow out of what they meant.

This is the pattern Jesus and the apostles actually modeled. In the New Testament, the leaders of the early Jesus communities were required to be "able to teach." But teach what? The Scriptures—meaning the Hebrew Bible, the very texts we now call the Old Testament. So we have to ask: if our modern interpretations minimize those Scriptures, override them, or interpret them through a lens foreign to their authors, are we truly teaching Scripture well? Or are we simply repeating the version that fits comfortably within our own worldview and tradition?

In a faith quick to echo the conclusions of others, we must learn to hear the biblical authors first—to honor the writer's voice before inserting our own. Later Christian interpretations are not invalid; they are part of the long and valuable conversation. But they are not the *only* conversation. Many of our inherited conclusions were formed within very different worlds, shaped by different questions and pressures than those faced by the first recipients of these texts. Recognizing that isn't dismissal. It's honesty. And it takes humility to ask whether the way we've reached our conclusions truly honors the ancient people who first received—and faithfully preserved—these words.

Most of us feel unqualified to read the Bible this way. But I see that as an advantage. We don't bring the lens of tradition or academia; we bring honest questions. We admit our disbelief. We come hungry and curious. And God delights in revealing himself to people like that— shepherds, fishermen, prostitutes, and exiles. If he can do it with them, why not with us too?

I realize this perspective sits in an unusual space. I stand as a non-Jewish follower of Jesus who has been shaped by an Evangelical faith, but who has come to see that faith in the light of a Jewish Messiah. My work is not an insider's defense of law observance, nor an outsider's critique of the church. It is an honest attempt to listen again to the voice of Scripture—to hear Leviticus as Jesus did, and to invite others, wherever they stand, to do the same.

THE CASE I'M MAKING

At the heart of this book are ten convictions:

1. Leviticus is dead because Christianity killed it. Our neglect, not Scripture's, has buried it.

2. Leviticus belongs to a story we no longer understand. It cannot be grasped apart from the covenant story of the first biblical books that frame it.

3. To understand Leviticus, we must understand the Messiah it reveals. Evangelical Christianity has built an image of Jesus largely without the story that defines him.

4. That Messiah is Jewish—and that matters. His identity and mission are bound to Israel and the Jewish people, not apart from it.

5. Both Jesus and the Prophets taught that Leviticus remains central to God's redemptive plan. Jesus has not yet fulfilled Leviticus in its fullest form, but continues to carry it toward its completion.

6. The apostles and earliest believers practiced Leviticus throughout their lives. They remained faithful, Torah-observant Jews while proclaiming Jesus as Messiah.

7. Paul and the apostles never taught that Leviticus was nullified—for anyone. They carried its instructions and standards into the communities they led.

8. The Letter to the Hebrews does not dethrone Leviticus. It teaches that Leviticus still stands—revealing its heavenly counterpart and affirming its continuing relevance on earth.

9. The new covenant does not replace Leviticus or supersede the old covenant. It renews and strengthens it, bringing its promises to fulfillment.

10. The absence of a temple today does not prove that God is done with Levitical worship. It testifies to God's covenant faithfulness—a pause in the story of temple worship, not its final conclusion.

These ten convictions may stretch how many of us were taught to read Scripture. They point to a vision in which Leviticus was never meant to fade into the background or be transformed into something else, but to keep unfolding until God's purposes reach their fullness in the Messiah. Jesus, the prophets, and the apostles all shared this view. The first followers of Jesus didn't abandon Levitical worship or dismiss its wisdom. For them, it revealed God's deepest desire: to dwell among his people.

Recovering that framework means asking hard questions that sometimes press against what we've inherited. But that tension is good—it invites us to bring our assumptions into the light so that Scripture's own worldview, not our traditions or systems, can reshape how we see God, Jesus, and the gospel. This book does not call for renewed ritual observance or the rejection of Christian tradition, but for a rediscovery of the gospel that Leviticus proclaims.

HOW TO READ THIS BOOK

Leviticus isn't a topic that most Christians pay much attention to—and that's exactly why I wrote this book. The first followers of Jesus knew Leviticus by heart. In first-century Judaism, Leviticus was the first book children began to learn—and they were excited about it. Why did Christians stop approaching it with that same eagerness? Somewhere along the way, we lost something.

This book is an attempt to recover what's been lost. It's not a verse-by-verse commentary or a call to keep every law in literal detail. It's an invitation to look again—to question the filters we've inherited and ask whether they've helped or hindered our understanding of God's Word. Theology, at its best, is both grief and grace. It asks you to hold what you've believed in one hand, and an uncomfortable truth in the other—and to see, with trembling honesty, where they no longer fit together. Rediscovering Leviticus takes curiosity to explore what's unfamiliar, humility to admit what we may have overlooked, and patience to let the story unfold on its own terms.

To make the journey accessible, I've written this book in plain language so that a reasonably committed reader can follow along with ease. For those who want to dig deeper, you'll find theological notes and extended discussions in the endnotes. Because this book challenges several long-standing Christian interpretations, I've also included an appendix exploring covenant, law, and the continuity of Scripture in greater depth. You don't need to read those sections to follow along—but they're there for anyone who wants to see the fuller case behind it and how my perspective fits within the wider landscape of Christian theology.

WHO THIS BOOK IS FOR

This book is written primarily for Evangelicals. My argument and critique are directed mainly toward Protestant Evangelical norms. That's the world I come from, and the one I most want to challenge. Yet the insights here reach beyond denominational boundaries. Catholic, Orthodox, and other Protestant readers will also find value in these pages because the questions raised by Leviticus touch every follower of Jesus.

It's also written for ordinary readers—people who love the Bible, wrestle with questions, and want to understand God's story more deeply. I believe you don't need a seminary degree or a stack of commentaries to read the Bible faithfully. God didn't inspire his Word for the spiritually or academically elite; he gave it to normal people learning to live it out together in community. Teachers, pastors, and scholars play a vital role in helping us handle Scripture responsibly—and we need responsible guidance now more than ever. My hope is that this book welcomes both the curious reader and the student of Scripture—anyone willing to listen for what the text itself has to say.

A BRIEF LOOK AT LEVITICUS

Before we dive in, it helps to know where we're headed and to recall what Leviticus actually contains. (Chapter 2 also provides a deeper look.) Leviticus sits at the very center of the first five books of Scripture, between the construction of the tabernacle in Exodus and Israel's wilderness journey in Numbers. It answers one central question: how can a holy God dwell among an unholy people?

In its pages, God prescribes a pattern of worship—both for the priests who represent Israel and for ordinary Israelites who host God's presence among them. The chapters of Leviticus form a rhythm of nearness, repentance, and renewal:

- Ritual Sacrifices (1–7): How God's people draw near to him through offerings.

- Priestly Ordination and Early Service (8–10): Priests set apart for sacred service.

- Ritual Purity Instructions (11–15): Keeping God's camp pure amid the realities of human life and decay.

- The Day of Atonement and the Call to Holiness (16–17): The centerpiece of Leviticus: holiness flowing out from the tent to the people.

- Moral Purity and Community Ethics (18–20): Guarding the holiness and shaping the ethics of the community that hosts God's presence.

- Qualifications for Priests (21–22): Upholding higher standards for those who minister in God's house.

- Sacred Times and Feasts (23–25): Remembering God's rhythm of redemption and meeting him on his own calendar of sacred time.

- Covenant Faithfulness and Blessings (26–27): The fruit of loyalty, love, and enduring devotion.

Everything in Leviticus revolves around the gift of God's presence—how it's made possible, protected, and celebrated. Far from an ancient rulebook, it's the blueprint for what it means to be a people among whom God dwells and how to host his presence well.

OPENING OUR MINDS

Two thousand years ago, two ordinary men trudged along the dusty road from Jerusalem to a small village called Emmaus. Their hearts were heavy, their minds racing, caught up in conversation about a man named Jesus of Nazareth—a rabbi who had stunned all of Israel. He had performed miracles that defied belief and taught the Hebrew Scriptures in ways no one ever had. Many were convinced that he was the promised Redeemer. And yet, the authorities had seized him and condemned him to death: their hopes seemed dashed.

As they walked, the resurrected Jesus joined them, though they did not recognize him at first. He listened quietly for a while, then said, "You are so slow to believe what the Hebrew Scriptures say! Don't you know that the Messiah must suffer all this before entering into his glory?" Then, step by step, he opened their minds. He showed them how the Scriptures pointed to the Messiah and revealed the fullness of God's story in ways they had never seen.

Jesus didn't first appear to scholars, teachers, or those with religious credentials. He sought ordinary men and women—those asking hard questions, those who were confused, unsettled, or sensing that they might have missed something. He opened the minds of curious, everyday people who simply wanted to know the truth about who he was and what the Scriptures actually said.

The Spirit our Lord left us with works in the same way today. If we approach Scripture with humility, ask the hard questions, and read through the lens Jesus used—the lens given to him by the Old Testament—he is faithful to open our minds too. Just as he did for the disciples on the road to Emmaus, he will help us see the story God has been telling all along.

Leviticus is central to that story. Like our resurrected Master, Leviticus is a living and ongoing part of God's redemptive plan, working in harmony with Jesus and shaping the faith of his people across every generation. We can learn to hear its voice and let it speak.

1

LEVITICUS IS DEAD

THIS BOOK WILL NEVER SELL A MILLION COPIES. I'll be lucky if it sells any at all. People don't read Leviticus, much less books about it. Leviticus simply doesn't matter to most Christians today. It's a dead book. We skim over it when we read the Bible in a year—if we don't just skip it entirely. Maybe you've felt that grind: reading about sacrifices you don't understand, purity laws that seem irrelevant, festivals you've never celebrated. You wonder, *What does any of this have to do with me?* Like Latin, it's preserved, occasionally quoted, even respected. But in practice, it's irrelevant to everyday faith.

A pastor once told me, "No one studies Leviticus in small groups—because no one shows up!" I've seen the same reaction in Bible studies. The minute someone suggests Leviticus, eyes glaze over, people shift in their chairs, and someone inevitably says, "Can't we just do James or Philippians instead?" We don't even give it a chance—we assume that we already know it's irrelevant. It feels strange, too ceremonial, too bound to an ancient people. At best, it's a relic we pull out to highlight how different we are from "Old Testament religion." At worst, it sits ignored, as if it has nothing left to say about faith any longer. That's how many of us encounter Leviticus. Not by reading it—but by *not* reading it. It disappears in plain sight. It's canonized, memorialized, liturgized, useful for context, but dead.

And we killed it.

CHRISTIANS DON'T UNDERSTAND LEVITICUS

My son's algebra teacher loves to say, "The reason you hate math is because you don't understand it." She's right—and not just about math. When we don't understand something, it feels intimidating, frustrating, and pointless. That's Leviticus. We don't avoid it because it's hard; we avoid it because no one's shown us why it matters.

We gravitate toward what feels familiar—justice, faith, forgiveness, discipleship. Pastors preach those themes, authors write on them, small groups discuss them. They feel relevant because someone has already cleared a path.

But Leviticus? It almost never comes up in church, let alone everyday Christian life. So if no one teaches it and no one talks about it, what chance does the average believer have of understanding it?

Here's the truth: Leviticus isn't impossible. Yes, it's repetitive. Yes, the rituals feel foreign. But a commentary can explain the details. The deeper problem is the label we've attached to it: irrelevant. We stamped it "expired at the cross" or "transformed by new traditions," so we don't even try to understand it.

No pastor we trust has shown us how to walk through it. No author we admire has cast a vision for why it matters. No small group has wrestled with its pages. We have no footsteps to follow, no trail markers, no one saying, *This is worth your time.* So the book stays shut—not because it's complicated, but because no one has shown us why it matters anymore.

PASTORS DON'T PREACH IT

In thirty years of church attendance, I've never heard a sermon series on Leviticus. Not once. Leviticus doesn't fill seats. Pulpits favor the Gospels, the New Testament letters, a life-of-David series. Even Genesis gets some airtime once in a while. But Leviticus? Silence. And silence shapes how people in the pews treat the book.

Even when pastors know it matters, the default is to preach the New Testament. Data confirm it: sermons lean thirty percent more toward the New Testament, even though the Old makes up roughly seventy-five percent of our Bibles.[1] The message is clear—the New Testament is the real food of our faith. In contrast, books like Leviticus are treated like multivitamins—nice if you have them, but definitely not essential.

In theory, we affirm the Old Testament as God's Word. In practice, we sideline it. And Leviticus? It isn't just on the margins; it's practically invisible. Silence in the pulpit produces ignorance in the pews. If pastors won't preach it, Christians won't read it.

CHRISTIANITY ASSUMES THAT JESUS REPLACED IT

The issue isn't simply that pastors prefer easier texts or congregations like familiar themes. There's a deeper assumption lurking under the silence. Many Christians believe that Jesus rendered Leviticus obsolete. He may have wanted us to preserve its morals, but its ceremonies, holy days, and rituals? Those, we assume, were fulfilled or simplified into other modes of worship we practice now. For most of us, that assumption takes one of two forms.

In more traditional and liturgical settings, Leviticus is seen as transcended—its sacrifices and priests fulfilled in Christ himself, then rewritten and fully realized in the sacraments. The altar becomes the table, the sacrifices become the Eucharist, the priesthood is spiritualized and replaced by clergy. Leviticus isn't rejected; it's transformed—honored and revered in memory but expressed through different forms of worship.[2]

In many Protestant traditions, Leviticus is seen as divided—its laws neatly sorted into moral, civil, and ceremonial categories. The moral commands still stand (at least in theory), but the rest are treated as temporary, belonging to ancient Israel's national and temple life. By this logic, Jesus fulfilled the "civil and ceremonial" parts, leaving only moral principles—usually reduced to love of God and neighbor—to follow.[3]

Both views were formed with sincere reverence, and many Christians find themselves straddling aspects of both. Each tried to make sense of Leviticus in light of the cross and each view arose within valid historical pressures. Yet in different ways, they share the same outcome: Leviticus is set aside. Whether elevated into new traditions or sorted into relevant and irrelevant, the book itself is lost because our traditions have told us that it has been replaced. In our minds, Leviticus has served its purpose. We have other ways of explaining it, even if those ways are foreign to Leviticus itself.

So if Christ's sacrifice made Levitical priests, rituals, and sacrifices irrelevant, why bother slogging through its ancient laws week after week from the pulpit? Why bother really engaging with it? It's already been decided. That quiet belief has shaped how we handle the Old Testament as a whole. We love Psalms for comfort, Isaiah for encouraging prophecy, Genesis for the big origin stories—but when the text sounds like law or ritual, we tune it out. We assume it's outdated. *Jesus took care of all that.*

Leviticus is the poster child for the "fulfilled and forgotten" mentality. The pulpit stays quiet. The congregation stays uninformed. The book stays closed. And the cycle rolls on, until it's lifeless in our hands. We inherit the assumption that it doesn't matter, and pass that assumption down to the next generation.

THE CYCLE OF NEGLECT IS KILLING LEVITICUS

That assumption let me justify my neglect of Leviticus. I hid behind the familiar Evangelical one-liners:

- *Jesus's sacrifice replaced animal offerings. Just offer your life.*

- *The new covenant fulfilled the Mosaic covenant.*

- *Christ kept the law, freeing us from it.*

- *Temple worship was temporary. Jesus is the real High Priest. We are now the temple.*

- *Leviticus teaches good principles, but its system is obsolete.*

Somewhere along the way, we shoved Leviticus aside and set Jesus right into its place. We imported him into every ritual, stamped *obsolete* across the whole scroll, and declared the conversation over. Leviticus flatlined in our imagination. Worse, we convinced ourselves that even dabbling in its rhythms—honoring its festivals, observing its purity laws, reclaiming its temple vision—threatens our faith in Jesus, as though valuing Leviticus somehow adds to his finished work on the cross or diminishes our own traditions.

In mainstream Christianity, anyone who treats Leviticus as vital is viewed as outside the box—more often, outside the lines—of accepted Christian practice. Sabbath at sundown on a Friday night? A Passover seder? Fasting on the Day of Atonement? Blowing a trumpet to open worship? These are God-ordained traditions. Jesus kept them. So did the apostles. Yet today they're often met with raised eyebrows, whispered accusations of "legalism," or outright dismissal: *Those are old priestly rules, irrelevant under grace. We're free from the law!*

And so the cycle spins. We affirm Leviticus as Scripture but ignore it in practice. Assumption becomes habit, habit hardens into tradition, and the book dies a little more—right inside our Bibles.

JESUS DIDN'T TREAT IT THAT WAY

But Jesus didn't treat Leviticus in this way. The book shaped every corner of our savior's life. He practiced its rituals and joined with Israel in everything it prescribed. He quoted its commands on love of neighbor, obeyed its laws on holiness, and learned its wisdom from the priests who taught him as a boy. For Jesus, Leviticus was not a dead scroll waiting to be retired by his actions. It was a living guide to God's mission and his own identity. It framed the hope of the redemption that he proclaimed.

The tragedy for us is that every time we sideline Leviticus, we dim the light on the gospel that Jesus actually preached. We distance ourselves from who Jesus says that he is. We tell ourselves we're protecting people from an irrelevant ritual or from falling into the legalism that the apostles condemned. But what we're really doing is cutting out the context that the Master's life and mission was built on.

This is a huge problem. If we claim to love Jesus and we stake our lives on his work, shouldn't we care about the book that shaped his life and work? What if our assumption—"Leviticus doesn't matter because Jesus replaced all those things"—is exactly backward? What if our neglect of Leviticus has so spoiled our appetite for the book that we don't even realize what we are missing?

As we move forward, we must confront how our reading of Scripture has shaped our understanding—or misunderstanding—of God, the Messiah, and his mission. Too often, we have approached the Bible through a lens that leaves the early books of the Bible weakened and Leviticus unread. When we do, we sever our faith from the very soil it first grew in—the revelation God already gave to Israel—and lose sight of the authority that shaped Jesus and the apostles. In the chapters ahead, we'll explore three key ways in which our vision has been distorted:

- How losing sight of the Torah leaves us unaware of the story God is telling

- How the Jesus we think we know obscures the Messiah that Scripture actually presents

- How being blind to what Jesus loves warps the gospel we proclaim

Each chapter will ask hard questions: are we following God while ignoring the path he laid out in Scripture? Do we really know Jesus as the Messiah he claims to be, or just the version our assumptions about him have created? Are we actually loving what he loves—or just what fits comfortably in our story? And how do we read Jesus and Leviticus so that they make sense together, within the bigger story?

This book exists to ask those questions, to disrupt the cycle of neglect, and to help us see Leviticus as Jesus did. Not as an artifact under glass that he retired, but as the heartbeat of the story that reveals the Messiah we love, the kingdom we are part of, and the gospel he proclaimed. The Hebrew title of Leviticus, *Vayikra*, means "And He Called." Today Leviticus is still calling. With the help of our Master, we can revive its message.

2

LOST WITHOUT THE TORAH

BEFORE WE CAN RECLAIM LEVITICUS, we have to reclaim something bigger—because Leviticus is part of something bigger. So if we want to understand Leviticus like Jesus did, then we have to start with a much larger question: what story do we think the Bible is telling?

Ten years ago, I'm not sure I could have answered that question clearly. I would have said what most Evangelicals say:

- *It's God's plan of redemption.*

- *It's our guidelines for living a faithful life in service of a holy God.*

- *It's about God and us, the problem of sin, and how forgiveness in Jesus secures eternal life.*

- *It's God's guidance to help us navigate life and grow in faith.*

I'm forever grateful for those messages—they brought me to where I am today. But eventually, they didn't go far enough. If the Bible was simply there to guide, encourage, and rescue me from sin, then why did so much of it seem so irrelevant? Judges? Leviticus? Obadiah? How did these connect to *my* walk with God? What did they have to do with my salvation?

In his book *The King Jesus Gospel*,[4] New Testament scholar Scot McKnight raises a piercing question: is the gospel we've been told the same gospel Jesus actually taught? He describes a salvation culture that centers on admitting sin, believing that Jesus died for us, and then "getting saved." That was the gospel that brought me to faith. I'm deeply grateful for it, but it wasn't the gospel Jesus proclaimed from the start of his ministry. And it isn't a gospel that leaves room for Leviticus.

THE PYRAMID PROBLEM

For me, the salvation culture gospel became a real problem. It was a great message for helping me to see my sin and to understand that I needed God's forgiveness. I believed in God, trusted my savior, and embraced a biblical worldview. I'd been taught that the Bible was mostly about my salvation and pleasing God with my life. But most of what I read—including Leviticus—didn't fit that story. How could a book about priests and sacrifices help me be a better Christian? What did something like Judges have to do with my salvation? I couldn't even summarize the minor prophets, let alone see how something like Obadiah mattered. Sure, I could quote a verse about God raising me up on eagles' wings from Isaiah—but I couldn't tell you what the rest of the book was about, or why Isaiah needed sixty-six chapters to make his point.

I came to faith believing that Jesus wanted to save me from my sins, and that the Bible was about how he did that. But most of what was actually in the Bible didn't have anything to do with those things. The problem wasn't God or Scripture—it was my expectations of what I was reading. Looking back, I'd been reading the Bible using what I refer to as a "pyramid strategy":

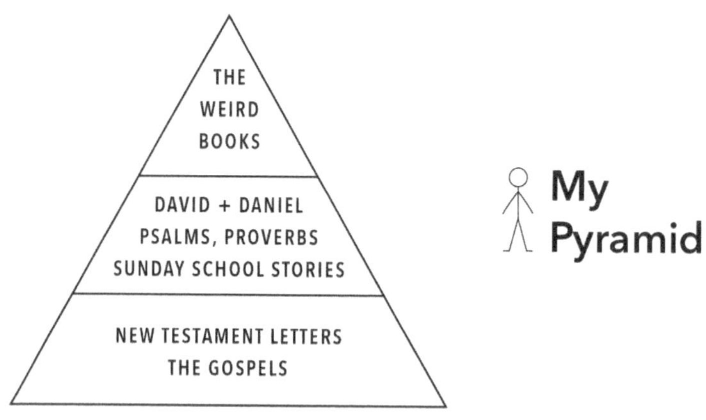

THE BASE: The Gospels—these were my foundation, my bread and butter. They told me about Jesus. And since loving Jesus was the most important thing for me to do as a Christian, the Gospels were clearly the most important part of the Bible. Just above them sat the New Testament letters: Romans, Ephesians, James. These books explained sin, salvation, and faith, and gave me rules for building a good, Christian life.

THE MIDDLE: The middle of the pyramid contained other things, less important, but still good to know. This was where I placed the Sunday school heroes, Psalms, Proverbs, and upbeat prophetic verses—encouraging, relatable, and easy to apply. I assumed that people like Abraham, Daniel, and David were models of faith, and so I tried to emulate them.

THE TOP: Everything else teetered on the top of the pyramid. Leviticus, Song of Songs, Habakkuk, Revelation—certainly part of Scripture, but unread. Sadly, the top of my pyramid contained the vast majority of the Bible.

This was how I saw Scripture modeled in all kinds of churches and in Bible studies, so it's how I read it myself for most of my life. I focused on what felt relevant to me—my problems, my salvation—and quietly ignored the rest. But eventually that strategy collapsed under its own weight. Whole books of the Bible sat unopened, unexplored, and unexplained, and I began to wonder why on earth these books were in Scripture if no one in Christianity ever bothered to use them?

But the more I ignored them, the louder the question became: why are these books even here? If they were truly part of God's inspired Word, why did almost no one in the church ever read or teach them? What if the parts I'd dismissed were actually the key to understanding the whole Bible?

Out of that frustration came a question that cracked everything open: *How did Jesus read these books? Do I understand my Bible the way he did?*

Those questions change everything because once you ask them, you can't help but notice how different Jesus's answer is from the one most of us have been taught.

JESUS'S FUNNEL

On the road to Emmaus, the risen Jesus said to two discouraged disciples: "'O foolish ones, and slow of heart to believe all that the prophets have spoken! Was it not necessary that the [Messiah] should suffer these things and enter into his glory?' And beginning with [the Torah] and all the Prophets, he interpreted to them in all the Scriptures the things concerning himself" (Luke 24:25–27). Jesus said that the Scriptures were about the Messiah—and that he was that Messiah. But what Jesus claimed the Bible was about was not at all how I had been taught how to read it.

Sometimes I used the Bible like a reference book for sin, justification, and other churchy words. Other times it was a moral handbook for "doing God's will." Sometimes it was my devotional mystery bag—pull a random verse, reflect, pray, move on. The Bible is useful, at times, for those things. But none of them are what Jesus said the Bible is about. And here's the kicker: none of those strategies work for books like Leviticus. You can't check off its rituals, use it like a theological dictionary, or reduce it to moral lessons. It has a story to tell, and it's one we've largely forgotten how to hear.

The reality is that there's a huge gap between how we most often approach the Bible and how Jesus did. We are not reading it through the same lens. The way we've learned who Jesus is and what he came to do is nothing like the way he learned about himself.

Where my pyramid left most of the Old Testament untouched, Jesus started wide with the Torah, then filtered through the Prophets and Writings to tell a unified story of the Messiah. His approach looked more like a funnel:

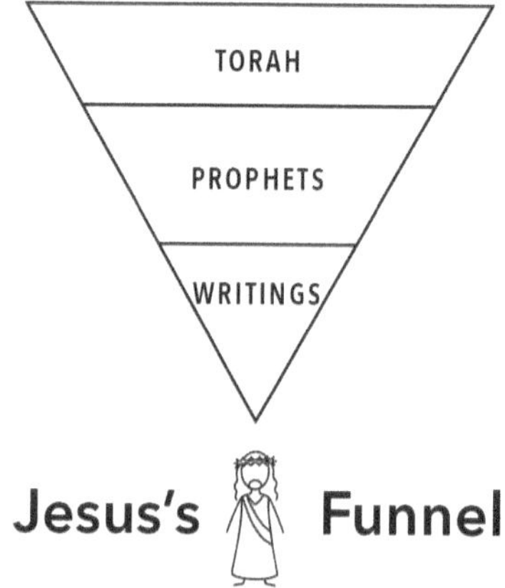

The approach of placing the New Testament as the base while leaving the Torah teetering at the top is the opposite of Jesus's approach. For him, everything began with the five books that open the Bible:

"*Beginning with [the Torah]* and all the Prophets, he interpreted to them in all the Scriptures the things concerning himself" (Luke 24:25–27).

Books like Leviticus weren't side-notes to Jesus. They were *essential* when he needed to explain himself. They defined him. I can't picture him unrolling the scroll of Leviticus only to explain how it would soon be set aside—simplified, voided, or repackaged into something easier for Christians to keep. He wasn't launching a new religion or rejecting the old one. He didn't view the temple system as outdated. Corrupt, yes—but replaceable? No. For Jesus, Leviticus wasn't an inadequate system he needed to fix. It was part of his identity.

Luke even gives us a glimpse of twelve-year-old Jesus in the Jerusalem temple, sitting among the teachers. He wasn't born with the Torah preloaded in his mind. Like every Jewish boy, he learned its stories, memorized its commands, and asked questions until he understood. Year by year, he grew into its identity.

For Jesus, the Torah was the primary lens for life. Everything revolved around it. His parents raised him inside its teachings—singing its songs, keeping its festivals, offering sacrifices—just as their parents had. The Hebrew Scriptures gave the words and vision to define his role as God's Anointed.

For years, I read the Gospels to learn about Jesus, and the apostles' letters to learn how to follow him better. But for Jesus, the Torah was enough. Leviticus and the other scrolls gave him all he needed to know about who he was and how to live faithfully. On the road to Emmaus, it was the Torah where he began, explaining everything about himself to ordinary people, just like you and me.

WHAT IS THE TORAH?

If the Torah was so central to Jesus, then we have to ask the obvious question: what is this Torah that shaped our Master? "Torah" simply means instruction or guidance. It names the first five books of the Bible— Genesis, Exodus, Leviticus, Numbers, Deuteronomy—but it also carries a broader sense. It is God's righteous standard, wisdom for his people.

The Torah is a connected story told across five scrolls, laying out what God wants to do in creation and how he plans to accomplish it. Its themes set the stage for everything else. The Torah is the hub of Scripture. Everything else in the Bible tries to link back to those early stories. So if we don't know the Torah—its stories, commands, and narrative—we will likely misread what comes after it. Genesis gives beginnings, Exodus tells of deliverance, Numbers and Deuteronomy carry the story forward, and at the center, like a heartbeat, sits Leviticus.

The Hebrew books of the Torah are crafted with artistic precision, structured as a *chiasm*, like a literary mountain, with Leviticus at the summit. In a chiasm, the outer components frame a central core. That core is the high point, the takeaway the author wants you to savor. In the Torah, Genesis and Deuteronomy form the slopes, while everything else builds toward—or descends from—the central summit.

Old Testament scholar Michael Morales argues that Leviticus is the peak of that mountain.[5] And not just any part of Leviticus: chapter 16, describing the Day of Atonement, sits at the center of both Leviticus and the Torah as a whole.[6] Simply put, Leviticus is the climax of the story. Jesus saw it as the pinnacle, the place the entire Torah had been leading.

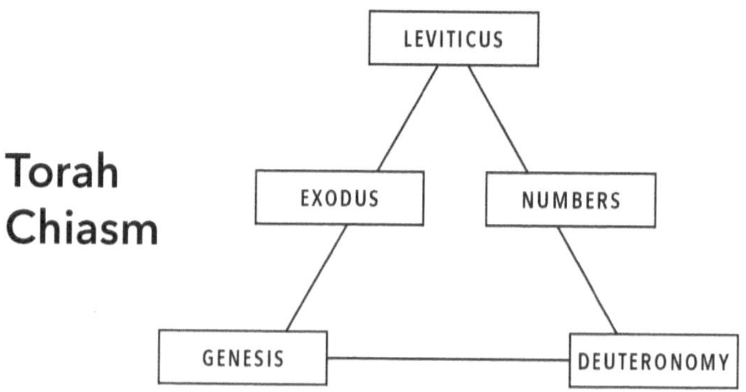

This mountain image shows why Leviticus matters. It isn't a detour or filler book. It is the pivot, the place where God explains how life with him actually works. Atonement, holiness, sacrifice, worship, celebration—all converge here. If we want to know what it means to rule as God's image, to be holy as he is holy, to love our neighbor, to draw near and worship God, the Torah points us to Leviticus.

Most Christians look for answers to these sorts of questions in places like the Sermon on the Mount, the Gospels, or Paul's letters. But the New Testament didn't invent the ideas we have about faithful living. Those authors inherited them from the Torah. Jesus and the apostles read these books as one coherent story, shaping every word they spoke.

We, on the other hand, rarely turn to the Torah to answer questions about Jesus or what he taught. This leaves us struggling. Trying to follow him without knowing the Torah is like trying to build a house starting on the second floor: the walls may go up, but there's no foundation beneath them.

Climbing to the Summit of the Torah—The Story of Leviticus
Picture the Torah as a mountain. Genesis and Deuteronomy form the long slopes on either side, Exodus and Numbers climb higher toward the center, and at the very top—where the air thins out and heaven meets earth—stands Leviticus. At the summit of the Torah, we're invited to stand still and listen. God's voice is about to speak from the tent.

At the end of Exodus, God's glory floods the tabernacle so powerfully that even Moses cannot enter. The question hangs in the air: *how can mortal people live this close to the blazing author of life?* From the first words of Leviticus, the point is clear: You can draw near. Its sacrifices, priestly ministry, and purity rituals are not hoops to jump through to earn God's favor. They form a pathway into life itself. Leviticus maps out what it means to dwell in the presence of a holy God.

Sacrifice—The Way Back
Leviticus opens with a new language of closeness in chapters 1–7: burnt,

grain, fellowship, sin, and guilt offerings. To us, it can sound like an ancient puzzle—sacrifices, blood, smoke? But to Israel it was good news. Each lamb laid on the altar, every splash of blood, each handful of flour carried the same quiet promise: death is not the final word. God himself has opened a way back into his presence.

Priesthood—Standing in the Gap

Next, chapters 8–10 unveil the priests. Washed, robed, anointed, they are more than temple staff; they are mediators, carrying Israel's gifts into God's presence and returning with his blessing. Their very lives act out Israel's calling to be a kingdom of priests—a light to the nations. Yet Aaron's sons failed almost immediately. The question lingers: when will there be a priest who can truly stand before God and not fail?

Purity—Choosing Life

Then the story shifts into chapters 11–15, a world of clean and unclean animals, odd skin checks, and rules about blood and birth. To us it sounds foreign, but the point is simple: life and death are not casual things. Every human bears the marks of mortality, and anyone carrying reminders of death cannot simply stroll into the presence of the living God. Ritual impurity isn't sinful—it's the natural result of living, bleeding, giving birth, and burying the dead. The danger is dragging those symbols of death into the space where only life belongs. So Israel learns to name what is holy, what is common, what signals mortality, and what protects the nearness of the God who gives life. These laws are not barriers but pathways, allowing people to draw close without polluting the place where God lives among them.

The Peak—Day of Atonement

Then comes chapters 16 and 17—the highest peak of the whole book. Once a year the high priest passes through the veil with sacrificial blood, cleansing Israel and resetting God's camp as pure again. A second goat is sent into the wilderness, carrying away the people's guilt. *Atonement* (*kippur*) means to purge or purify, clearing human residue so God's presence can remain among his people. Think of a kitchen: every meal leaves scraps and peelings. Without someone to clear the counters and take out the trash, the whole space quickly becomes foul. Atonement is God's built-in cleanup system, keeping his house pure among impure mortals. Even the altar needs atonement—not because it sins, but because impurity clings to everything humans touch. "It is the blood that makes atonement for one's life" (17:11, NIV). Leviticus tells the story of life continually chasing death away so God can remain in the center of his people.

Holiness Every Day
From there, Leviticus 18–25 spreads holiness into Israel's families, homes, and culture—sexual integrity, honest scales, justice for the poor, Sabbath rest, jubilee release. "Be holy, for I am holy" was no suggestion—it's a command. Holiness is to touch every part of life.

A Call to Covenant Faithfulness
Leviticus concludes in chapters 26–27 with a promise and a warning: if Israel walks this way, blessing will overflow; if they turn away, the cost will be exile and death. As the story moves down the mountain into Numbers and Deuteronomy, the question remains: will Israel uphold God's ways and host his presence faithfully?

WHY LEVITICUS MATTERS

For many of us, that question barely registers. In fact, you may have even skimmed over that entire section. Nothing in these past few paragraphs appears to have anything to do with you and me. We've already settled in our minds that Israel failed and that Jesus freed us from ever needing Leviticus again. If the story of Leviticus ends in failure anyway, why linger over details that we assume were cancelled by Jesus at the cross? For most Christians, the answer seems straightforward: Jesus brought Leviticus to an end. Its meaning is gathered up in him—its sacrifices fulfilled, its priests and rituals replaced by new forms of worship. The moral core survives, but the rest? We've moved on, convinced Leviticus has done its job and moved offstage.

But what if Jesus answers that question differently? What if he sees an ending we've missed—not through a crystal ball, but because he knows the Torah and the Prophets? Jesus grew up inside the story of Leviticus. He lived in it, died in it, and now reigns in it—and his work within that story is not finished. But because we've dismissed the central book of in the story of the Torah, we're left trying to fit a Jesus we don't really know into a story we don't understand. We've built our picture of Jesus apart from the Torah. We severed him from the very books he used to define his own mission and identity.

That's why we turn to Hebrews or the New Testament to explain Leviticus. We can't see how it fits in harmony alongside Jesus because we haven't learned to hear the story in the same way he did, or guard its meaning with the same devotion. Jesus didn't read Leviticus to check its boxes or replace it with himself. He let it speak, allowing its story to shape his life. Every Sabbath he kept, every festival he celebrated, every prayer he prayed—everything was shaped by Torah.

If the Torah was the heartbeat of Jesus's gospel, and Leviticus is the heart of the Torah, how can we know Jesus—or his gospel—without it? If we're honest, most of us couldn't explain the gospel through Leviticus. We've let it die at the top of our pyramids, dismissing it as law replaced by grace or new traditions. That's because most of us read the Bible as a story about us: our sin, our forgiveness, our lives, our path to heaven.

But Leviticus isn't about us—it's the Torah's heart and the story Jesus lived in. Without it, we're lost. Without Leviticus, our gospel isn't Jesus's gospel. Today if you asked me what the Bible was about, my response would sound very different than it would have ten years ago: The Bible is a unified story about a God—Yahweh—who wants to partner with humans to rule his creation through a covenant mediated by the Messiah of Israel, Jesus of Nazareth.[7] Jesus and the apostles read the Scriptures this way—as a single story leading to a Messiah. For them, that story began in the Torah. And Leviticus was at the heart.

If we truly love Jesus and want to follow him faithfully, then we must honor the Scriptures by learning to understand them as he did. We ought to know what he believed it meant to be the Messiah—and what truly mattered to him—not just what we assume.

This shift invites a different kind of journey with the Bible than most of us are used to, but it's a journey that draws us closer to the heart of the Father. And that journey begins with the Torah: climbing to its summit, pausing, and listening—truly listening—to the story Leviticus has been telling all along.

3

A JESUS WE THINK WE KNOW

IF LEVITICUS IS THE SUMMIT OF THE TORAH, then Jesus is one we find standing on its top. Leviticus leaves us with a question: *Will God's people truly host his presence faithfully so he can live among them?* This question is answered in Jesus. He read Leviticus as a story that points to the Messiah. But the question is, do we?

Do we really know the Messiah Jesus claims to be? Or have we constructed our own version of Jesus solely from the stories we've read about his life? Often, we let the Gospel narratives drive our understanding of him—which is good, but they were never meant to stand alone. The Gospels were written to show why it is good news that Jesus is the Messiah the Hebrew Scriptures anticipated. But if we don't know the Messiah of the Hebrew Scriptures, then we have no hope of understanding Jesus for who he truly is.

The Torah shaped how Jesus and the gospel authors understood the Messiah, his mission, and his embodiment of God's promises. The Old Testament is full of portraits and promises, each revealing aspects of the Messiah's role. Without that foundation, his identity and purpose begin to fade. Leviticus, surprisingly, is one of the best tests of whether we grasp Messiah rightly precisely because it doesn't look messianic at first glance. For most of my life, I couldn't make the connection. Jesus believed that Leviticus pointed to him, but apart from the high priestly imagery and sacrifice for sin, I didn't see it. The problem wasn't with Leviticus. It was with my definition of "Messiah."

The truth is, I didn't know what "Messiah" actually meant. I knew *who* the Messiah was—Jesus—but I couldn't have explained the meaning of the word, what the role entailed, or outlined a biblical profile of the office. (I didn't even realize that Messiah *was* an office!) Without that foundation, I lacked the categories to read Leviticus as the messianic literature Jesus claimed it to be. Despite following Jesus and reading the Bible for nearly my entire life, I had much to learn about who he said he was—and how Leviticus fit into that story.

This chapter will not provide an exhaustive exploration of the Hebrew concept of the Messiah—that could fill an entire book. But if we take Jesus at his word, that Leviticus is about a Messiah, then we first need to know, specifically, what a Messiah is.

THE VAGUENESS OF "MESSIAH"

It's ironic: the term "Christian" literally means "follower of the Messiah." Yet most believers carry a fuzzy, mixed-up sense of what Messiah actually means. Here's what we usually assume:

- Messiah is a name for Jesus: We use "Christ" (from the Greek *christos*, meaning Messiah) interchangeably with Jesus: "Christ Jesus," "Jesus Christ," "Be like Christ." These phrases are so familiar we rarely notice the distinction. They are synonymous.

- Messiah is a personal savior: A figure who saves individuals from their sins.

- Messiah is a heroic rescuer: Pop culture sometimes uses it for someone who saves humanity from disaster (e.g., in the film *Deep Impact*, the spaceship sent to save Earth is called "The Messiah").

- Messianic as a sect: Refers to Jews who believe Jesus is the Messiah.

Even reference works like *Encyclopedia Britannica* reflect the confusion.[8] Depending on context, *Messiah* can mean a king from David's line who restores Israel, the historical Jesus of Nazareth, any redeeming figure, or even a vague adjective for end-times hopes. With such a wide range of meanings in play, it's no wonder Christians carry fuzzy, mixed-up ideas of what "Messiah" actually means.

One of Leviticus's main contributions to the Torah is its portrait of a *mashiach*—a messiah. The Hebrew term appears about fifteen times throughout the book, usually translated "anoint" or "anointed." That's what messiah means: "to anoint." And it's not just people. Throughout the Bible, lots of things get anointed. You could even call an anointed rock a "messiah," because the word simply means something set apart by oil. Anointing signals that whatever has been touched by oil is no longer ordinary—whether it's a king, a prophet, an altar, or the high priest himself. The moments where this happens in Leviticus aren't throwaway details. They're part of how the Torah builds its messianic theme and sketches the profile of the ultimate Messiah to come.

WHAT DOES JESUS THINK A MESSIAH IS?

Let's look at Jesus's own words. Throughout this book, wherever Scripture uses "Christ," I've replaced it with [Messiah] to keep the meaning front and center. *Christ* means Messiah, and Messiah is not a vague spiritual nickname. It's a precise role with specific responsibilities.

On the road to Emmaus Jesus told the disciples: "'O foolish ones, and slow of heart to believe all that the prophets have spoken! Was it not necessary that *the [Messiah]* should suffer these things and enter into his glory?' And beginning with [the Torah] and all the Prophets, he interpreted to them in all the Scriptures the things concerning himself" (Luke 24:25–27).

Notice what Jesus does *not* say. He doesn't tell them, "Wasn't it necessary that *I* suffer …?" Instead, he speaks of the Messiah in the third person—as a role, an office, a position with a mission. His given name is Yeshua—that's what his mother called him—but "Messiah" was his title, and that title came with specific expectations laid out in Scripture.

Think of it like "President." President isn't a person—it's an office with duties and authority. The private citizen Franklin D. Roosevelt didn't command the U.S. military during WWII, but President Roosevelt did. Likewise, Jesus's identity as a man is distinct from his office as the Messiah.

What's striking is how Jesus proves this point. He doesn't lean on his personal experience—he doesn't say, "I was crucified, now I'm alive again, so clearly I'm the Messiah." Instead, he guides them through Scripture, "beginning with Moses and all the Prophets." That phrase is shorthand for the Torah, the former Prophets (Joshua, Judges, Samuel, Kings), and the latter Prophets. Jesus walks them through the storyline of a Messiah who suffers before entering glory.

It amazes me that he lets the Scriptures do the heavy lifting. No dramatic reveal, no firsthand testimony of the cross. Instead, he roots the Messiah in the Hebrew Bible, showing that the Torah and Prophets had already spelled out the mission centuries earlier. The scrolls themselves bear the weight of his identity. Luke doesn't list which texts came up in that conversation. He doesn't need to. Like Jesus, Luke and the disciples already knew the Scriptures as a unified story about a God, Yahweh, uniting with humanity through a covenant mediated by a Messiah. For them, the entire Bible was messianic literature.

HOW THE TORAH DEPICTS MESSIAH

Although Jesus doesn't appear by name until the New Testament, the Torah is full of messianic undertones. Page after page, Yahweh partners with humans to advance his plan for creation. These covenant partners often live out the same pattern of suffering and exaltation that Jesus pointed to. Sometimes, they suffer:

- Noah, faithful in an age of judgment.

- Jacob, contending with enemies and even with God for blessing.

- Moses, offering his own life in place of Israel after the golden calf.

- Aaron, risking his life by running into a plague and restoring life to Israel.

At other times, they reign in glory:

- Melchizedek, priest-king, blessing Abram with bread and wine.

- Abraham, vindicated after obeying God on Mt. Moriah.

- Israel, hosting God's presence in the tabernacle.

- Joseph, whose life is the very pattern of messianic hope—suffering to save his family (and the nations), then rising to rule the known world.

The Torah also speaks in direct promises—prophecies that point forward to a coming human partner who will fully embody God's design for humanity:

- To Eve, God promises a descendant who will crush evil's head, though wounded in the process.

- To Abraham, a family line through whom all nations will be blessed.

- To Judah, a ruler's scepter and victory over his enemies.

- To Joseph, a fruitful branch bringing blessing to the world.

- Through Balaam, a star and scepter rising from Israel—an unstoppable king.

- In Leviticus, the high priest himself is called a *mashiach* ("messiah")—the anointed mediator between God and his people.

It's tempting to immediately read Jesus back into these stories. And yes, he fulfills them perfectly. But for Israel, these weren't random hints—they were building a job description of the Messiah: a human who would suffer faithfully, reign gloriously, and accomplish God's purposes.

HOW THE PROPHETS DEPICT THE MESSIAH

The prophets continue this same logic. In Samuel, God promises David and Solomon that a king from their line will reign forever in Jerusalem. David united the tribes, defeated enemies, and prepared the site for God's house. Solomon built the temple. These were messianic tasks. Even if they didn't complete them perfectly, David and Solomon do the job of a messiah.

Isaiah expands the picture with the suffering servant who bears burdens and heals, yet also rises in glory to restore his family. And Isaiah also envisions a ruling king (9:6–7):

> For to us a child is born,
>   to us a son is given;
>   and the government shall be upon his shoulder,
>   and his name shall be called
> Wonderful Counselor, Mighty God,
>   Everlasting Father, Prince of Peace.
> Of the increase of his government and of peace
>   there will be no end,
>   on the throne of David and over his kingdom,
>   to establish it and to uphold it
>   with justice and with righteousness
>   from this time forth and forevermore.
> The zeal of the LORD of hosts will do this.

In context, these famous Christmas Eve verses aren't about a baby in a manger. They describe the Messiah reigning in glory. The throne is David's in Jerusalem. The role is Jewish at its core.

As a kid in church on Christmas Eve, when I heard, "Unto us a child is born, unto us a son is given," I thought it meant, "Unto everyone who believes in Jesus, a child is born." The candles, carols, and warm glow made it feel addressed straight to me and my family. But Isaiah's "us" wasn't generic humanity. It was Israel. His "child" was their Messiah, promised to fulfill their covenant story. That doesn't exclude the rest of us. Isaiah and the other prophets are clear that the blessings of Messiah's reign will overflow to the nations. But the Messiah is Jewish, the promises are Jewish, and the throne is in Jerusalem. The Messiah is not a culturally neutral figure, but a Jewish king the Scriptures promise. The Messiah is Israel's king.

HOW THE PSALMS DEPICT THE MESSIAH

The Psalms are among the richest sources of messianic imagery in the Hebrew Bible. They combine human emotion with a vision that trusts in God's plan. Because they are poetry, they often condense vast ideas into just a few vivid lines. Many of these psalms—especially those attributed to David—speak of an anointed ruler, a priestly king, or a suffering but vindicated servant. They outline specific messianic roles rooted in Israel's hopes. Let's look at three portraits.

Portrait No. 1: Psalm 2—The Reign of Yahweh's Messiah

> Why do the nations rage … Kiss the Son, lest he be angry, and you perish in the way … Blessed are all who take refuge in him.

In this Psalm, the rulers of the earth unite against Yahweh and his anointed, but their rebellion is utterly futile. God has already established his king—his Messiah—on Zion. In the ancient Israelite context, "Son of God" was not about literal offspring but a royal, messianic title. Throughout the Bible, "son" can function as a synonym for Messiah. The titles *"Son of God"* and *"Son of David"* don't necessarily mean "child of God" in the way we might picture one of our own children. In Hebrew thought, *sonship* implied likeness, authority, and inheritance. The word *ben* ("son") often described one who carried another's image or represented another's rule. Kings of Israel were sometimes called *sons of God* because they ruled on his behalf (2 Samuel 7:14; Psalm 2:7). To call Jesus the *Son of David* is a way to say he is the promised heir to Israel's throne; to call him the *Son of God* identifies him as the one who would embody God's reign on earth. Both titles carried deep messianic weight.[9]

Psalm 2 presents a powerful image: a Messiah who shatters opposition like fragile pottery, yet offers blessing and refuge to those who turn to him. The nations are warned to pay homage because his rule is unbreakable, and his authority comes directly from Yahweh.

Portrait No. 2: Psalm 110—The One Who Sits at Yahweh's Right Hand
If Psalm 2 shows the Messiah enthroned over the nations, Psalm 110 invites us into the heavenly court to witness the source of his authority (author's translation):

> Yahweh says to my master: "Sit at my right hand until I make your enemies your footstool." … You are a priest forever after the order of Melchizedek.

In the Ancient Near East, the right hand of a ruler wasn't just a good seat—it was the place of highest trust and shared rule.[10] The one seated there acted with the king's authority in judgment, warfare, and administration. To sit at Yahweh's right hand is to be elevated to supreme authority, empowered to act with God's own strength.

David envisions the Messiah as both king and priest—a rare combination in Israel. Drawing on the Torah's account of Melchizedek, David portrays a Messiah who represents the people before God and subdues rebellious nations with decisive power. Yahweh himself stands at the Messiah's right hand in battle, a partnership that is unshakable and unstoppable.

In this Psalm, David was not necessarily foreseeing the pre-incarnate Jesus in a prophetic vision. More likely, his imagination was shaped by the messianic portraits he knew from the stories in the Torah. He fused traits from Melchizedek, Abram, and Moses into a single figure: a priestly king, a warrior, a deliverer. Psalm 110 portrays a Messiah whose authority is absolute, whose judgment is certain, and whose mission is inseparable from God's covenant promises.

Portrait No. 3: Psalm 22—The Forsaken One
Psalm 22 shows the Messiah at his lowest—forsaken, afflicted, yet ultimately vindicated:

> My God, my God, why have you forsaken me? … All the ends of the earth shall remember and turn to the LORD.

David likely wrote this during a personal crisis, fleeing enemies and seeking God's protection. Drawing on the messianic profile from the Torah, he described his own trials in messianic terms—seeing himself as an "anointed one" but pointing toward a greater Messiah yet to come. Jesus knew this Psalm well and identified with it on the cross, not merely quoting it as a prophecy of his current circumstance, but as a lens for understanding his suffering as Messiah and God's faithfulness to him.

David's cries are not private laments; they are public testimony. The "brothers" are Israel, the "congregation" is the worshipping nation, and even amid suffering, he trusts God has not abandoned his people or his Messiah.

All the ends of the earth shall remember and turn to the LORD, and all the families of the nations shall worship before you. For kingship belongs to the LORD, and he rules over the nations.

Through this, David frames the Messiah as God's chosen king, ruling not for himself but by divine appointment. The Scriptures present a Messiah who, like David, is enthroned. But this ultimate Messiah sits at God's right hand, waging victory, judging the rebellious, and bringing peace and restoration to Israel and the nations. Psalm 22 shows that even in apparent forsakenness, the Messiah's suffering is tied to God's ultimate plan to bless the world.

Christians are well acquainted with the Messiah as the suffering servant, a beautiful and true reality. Yet that suffering and death are only the opening act of his mission, occurring at the very start of his "term in office," so to speak. The far greater portion of Messiah's job centers not on dying, but on reigning—wielding divine authority to bring God's kingdom to the land.

I can't speak for everyone, but for me, this was a very different picture of Christ than Christianity ever gave me. These passages go far beyond the personal, loving shepherd, and gentle, forgiving savior I had always assumed Christ to be. That doesn't mean that the Messiah isn't those things. It means I had overlooked much of who *he* understood himself to be. In all my years of church life, I rarely heard these parts of Jesus's story emphasized. Sermons and studies focused on his divinity, his compassion, his victory over sin—but hardly ever on what it meant for him to be *Israel's Messiah*. I grew up knowing the Savior of the world, but not the Son of David who stands within Israel's story.

DID ISRAEL ONLY KNOW THE MESSIAH IN PART?

All of these Old Testament images present an interesting question: Did Israel really know who they were waiting for? It's commonly thought within Christianity that Israel's understanding of God and his Messiah was partial—present in shadow, but incomplete until Jesus came. According to this view, the Jews had only a hazy grasp of the Messiah until the brighter light of the New Testament revealed him fully. But Scripture tells a different story.

John writes, "He came to his own, and his own people did not receive him. But to all who did receive him, who believed in his name, he gave the right to become children of God" (John 1:11–12). From the start, John shows both rejection and reception within Israel—and the rest of his gospel bears that out.

When Jesus met the disciples on the road to Emmaus, he didn't unveil something new. As the master teacher he was, he simply revealed what had been there all along—showing that Moses and the Prophets had spoken plainly of him (Luke 24:27). No new text was needed, only renewed sight.

Throughout his life, ordinary Jews recognized him for who he was, sometimes without him saying a word. Simeon and Anna proclaimed him as Messiah when he was still an infant (Luke 2:25–38). Philip announced to Nathanael that he had found the Messiah—the very one Moses and the Prophets had written about—and Nathanael quickly confessed to Jesus, "You are the Son of God, the King of Israel" (John 1:49). Peter declared him the Messiah (Matthew 16:16), and Martha echoed the same faith (John 11:27). Blind men cried out, "Son of

David!" (Matthew 20:30–31), and crowds hailed him with those same words as he entered Jerusalem (Matthew 21:9). Children in the temple shouted his praise (Matthew 21:15–16). Even Nicodemus—an educated Pharisee—confessed, "Rabbi, we know You are a teacher come from God," and later honored him at his burial with spices fit for a king (John 3:2; 19:39). From rabbis to laborers, Israel was full of people who recognized their Messiah long before his resurrection.

Even Gentiles saw him through Israel's Scriptures: magi who followed a prophetic star, a centurion who trusted his word, a Canaanite woman who called him *Son of David*, a Samaritan woman who awaited Messiah, and a Roman soldier who named him *Son of God* at his death. Their faith didn't spring from new revelation but from recognizing a portrait from the Hebrew Bible unfolding before their eyes.

The idea that Israel possessed only a partial revelation of God doesn't arise from Scripture but from later Christian theology. It grew out of a framework that assumed the Church replaces Israel—a view the biblical authors themselves never held, because such an idea didn't yet exist. This view assumes the Old Testament was always dependent upon revelatory reinterpretation by the Church and the New Testament to shed full light on it. But that view forgets something vital. These were the very Scriptures Jesus himself used to understand his mission. These texts shaped his prayers, his parables, his compassion, and his calling. To imply they were insufficient overlooks the fullness already present in them—the same fullness that revealed the Messiah to many before a single gospel was ever written.

I recently heard the public testimony of a Jewish man who came to follow Jesus. By his own admission, he'd been a secular Jew—uninterested in religion, and increasingly irritated by Christians who kept trying to convert him. Finally, in exasperation, he went to his sister, a Jewish believer, and issued a challenge: *"Show me how Jesus is the Messiah, but do it without your Christian New Testament. Use only our Scriptures. And no personal stories—just the text."*

She agreed. As he recounted what happened next, his voice broke.

Page by page, she led him through the Hebrew Bible, showing him the portrait of the Messiah that had been there all along. He saw, in the words of his own heritage, the face of Jesus. Today, his story joins many others, a living testimony that God is still at work among the Jewish people through the Jewish Scriptures themselves, without the need for Christian enlightenment.

The earliest followers of Jesus needed no New Testament to recognize or proclaim him as the Messiah. Like that man searching his own Scriptures, they found him already there, in the promises they had known since childhood. Their understanding deepened through the Spirit's guidance as they continued to search the sacred texts—but that is the growth that Psalm 1 promises, the fruit of steady meditation, not enlightenment that rose above it or rewrote its meaning. The same Spirit who hovered over creation (Genesis 1:2) was still moving among them, illuminating what had always been true: the faithfulness of Israel's God unfolding before their eyes. Those first Jewish believers were part of the ongoing remnant who have recognized in Jesus what the prophets have declared all along.

FAITH WITHOUT A BIBLICAL PORTRAIT OF MESSIAH

For several years, our family has hosted a Passover seder, often inviting other believers to join us. It's a big event. Weeks of preparation go into the meal, the program, and the storytelling. We walk guests through each element, aiming to worship God by experiencing Jesus through the Passover. One year, after the seder ended, a guest sought me out. She was honored to have been invited, loved the beautiful meal and table decorations, and was surprised by how much she learned. But then she asked me an interesting question: "All this is wonderful, but when will you get back to really worshipping God? How do you make room in your life to just be in his presence and enjoy him—without all the Jewish stuff?"

At the time, I didn't quite understand her question. I'm sure I fumbled my way through a polite response. Looking back, I now see what she meant. This is a person who loves Jesus and has devoted her life to him, but she had no clue about his role as Messiah. The "Jewish stuff" at Passover was peripheral—not central—to her view of Jesus. Most of her perception about him stopped at the cross and resurrection. What more could he possibly have to do? In her mind, Jesus had already completed the entire messianic job description: live sinlessly, die sacrificially, conquer sin, rise from the grave, ascend to heaven.

But the ongoing role of the nation-ruling, judgment-wielding, government-establishing, peace-keeping Jewish Messiah? That wasn't even on her radar. She couldn't comprehend how the holiday of Passover is, still, real worship. In her defense, it is unusual for a non-Jewish family to host a Passover seder. But that gap says a lot about how we view worship. For my guest, it might as well have been the Fourth of July. She saw the festival as a quaint tradition, not as a biblically ordained act of devotion. It was hard for her to see that celebrating Passover isn't about becoming Jewish or reviving an ancient tradition for nostalgia. It's about seeing the Messiah the way the Bible describes him, and letting that vision become part of our lives through worship. Our guest couldn't see any of it—Leviticus, Passover, even Jesus himself—as messianic. She had no foundation for understanding what a Messiah really was.

FINAL THOUGHTS

It might seem like this chapter has wandered far from our mission to recover Leviticus. But how we understand Messiah shapes how we read the entire Bible. We cannot draw our picture of Jesus only from the New Testament. The one who gave his life for us understood himself through the Scriptures of Israel. He spoke their messianic words with his last breaths. Every New Testament author knew him through that same lens. Leviticus is not just part of that story. It is the center of it.

The assumption—that Leviticus consists merely of rules for an ancient people, expired at the cross—cuts the thread that runs from Eden to Sinai to Zion to the eternal throne. Too often we dismiss the rituals of Leviticus as relics, convinced that real worship must look more "biblical" or more "Christian" by our own definition. But in doing so, we pull Leviticus away from its messianic trajectory. What we shrug off as fulfilled, lifeless rituals, Jesus saw as the roadmap of his mission, the job description of the Messiah and shape of his destiny.

If we see Jesus as he saw himself—the Messiah of the Torah, Prophets, and Psalms—then Leviticus is no longer optional. It is *essential* to knowing the person we trust with our lives. On the road to Emmaus, Jesus didn't sketch a vague Christ-figure from the New Testament. He painted a very specific picture of the Old Testament Messiah—a portrait that included Leviticus. And then he showed that through his death and resurrection, he occupies that office.

That day, Jesus made clear what the Torah had been saying all along: the Scriptures are about a Messiah. In him, that ancient hope took flesh and began its long walk to fulfillment.

4

BLIND TO WHAT HE LOVES

IF WE BELIEVE THAT JESUS is truly the Messiah, and we claim to stake our lives on that, then we should know what matters to him. Not what we assume matters, not what feels most urgent to us, but what matters to him. What does the Messiah of Israel care about? Leviticus gives us a starting point. It reminds us where the Messiah's mission begins: with God's people and God's promises.

Understanding what is important to our Messiah is not optional. We cannot settle for a vague, sentimental view of his heart. Often, our picture of Jesus is drawn from popular stories about him: eating with the marginalized, healing the sick, loving the poor and downtrodden. Those things are true and instructive for us—but we forget the context. The poor, the marginalized, the suffering people he reached were, overwhelmingly, Jews. The tax collectors and sinners? Prostitutes and cripples? They were Jews living in Israel, under the standard of the Torah Jesus embraced and taught.

The things that matter most to the Messiah of Israel are the people and land of Israel. Jesus healed primarily Jewish individuals, taught in Jewish in synagogues and walked through towns and villages full of Jewish people (Matthew 9:35–36). He explicitly said he came for "the lost sheep of Israel" (Matthew 15:24), and the majority of his ministry took place within Israel's boundaries. Even when he ministered to Gentiles, these moments were exceptions, not the rule. Of the two biblical accounts we have of Jesus overcome with emotion, one of them is an intense scene where he is bitterly weeping over a city deeply important to him: Jerusalem. Our lord wept over the crown jewel of the land he represents as its Messiah (Luke 19:41–44). The heart of his messianic mission is deeply focused on and tied to the people and land of Israel.

THE UNIFIED STORY OF THE BIBLE HINGES ON A LINCHPIN

Christianity approaches the Bible as though it's a Christian book. We tend to read it as though it were written for our culture and traditions. This is why we struggle so much with Leviticus. It doesn't fit into that context. When we read the Bible, even when we say "Christ," we often picture Jesus as an ethnically ambiguous figure. But this is not how Jesus envisioned his role.

The Bible holds tremendous wisdom for us today, but it didn't arise from a Western (or Christian) worldview. It is an Israel-centric, Jewish-centric, Middle Eastern story from start to finish. And every single one of its sixty-six books are working together to tell that story. Pull one book out and the story begins to fray. That's exactly what we've done with Leviticus.

From the opening of Genesis, everything is rooted in God's relationship with one people: the descendants of Abraham. Through them, he promised to bless all nations. He accomplishes this plan through covenants with this family, overseen by their Messiah (the topic of a later chapter and an expanded discussion in the appendix).

In the previous chapter, I briefly highlighted the Jewish ethnicity of the Messiah and the Jewish nature of the office itself. From Genesis to Revelation, the role of the Messiah is intrinsically Jewish. If Jesus were not Jewish, he could not be the Messiah. His lineage, mission, and authority are anchored in Israel's story.

Believers often struggle with a simple truth: Jesus was not a Christian.[11] Jesus is Jewish. Not "Jew-ish," as if he is partly Jewish, but bent the rules of Judaism to invent a new faith. He did not stop being Jewish after the resurrection. He remains, to this day, a living, resurrected Jewish man, born to a Jewish mother, raised by Jewish parents in Israel. And the Bible teaches that he is returning to Israel to finish what he started.

The land of Israel and the Jewish people are at the heart of God's plan to redeem the world through his Messiah. Yet Christianity has often overlooked this, as if God's promises could be untied from the family to whom he first made them. God chose Abraham's line, promising that through them all nations would be blessed—and that promise has never been revoked.

Jesus was, and remains, fully Jewish. He didn't invent a new religion called Christianity, and his disciples didn't "convert" from Judaism. Jews who recognize him as Messiah are simply seeing what their own Scriptures always promised. For non-Jews like me, the revelation comes differently: we are actually learning to worship the God of Abraham and follow the Messiah of Israel. That does not make us Jewish, nor does it require conversion—but it does mean recognizing that the Messiah we follow and the God we worship is defined by and rooted in a very Jewish story.

This leads to an unavoidable truth about the Bible: its context is Israel-centric and Jewish-centric from beginning to end. Almost every book was written by Jews, for Jewish audiences, across centuries of history in and around the land of Israel. The biblical authors assumed that their readers would have no problem with Jesus being Jewish, with God's plan tied to the Jewish people, and with the land of Israel playing a central role.

That's hard for many of us. Most believers I know—including myself—struggle to read the Bible through that lens. We're not deliberately ignoring context; we simply know little about Israel or the Jewish people. Christian teaching has often downplayed this heritage, leaving us disconnected from the world in which Scripture lives. Recovering it goes far beyond learning geography, history, or religious customs. It means recognizing that we are outsiders stepping into someone else's sacred story. The Scriptures we cherish are first and foremost Israel's story, rooted in a Jewish identity. As Christians, we have been graciously grafted into their story—not the other way around.

> And you Gentiles, who were branches from a wild olive tree, have been grafted in. So now you also receive the blessing God has promised Abraham and his children, sharing in the rich nourishment from the root of God's special olive tree. But you must not brag about being grafted in *to replace* the branches that were broken off. You are just a branch, not the root. (Romans 11:17–18, NLT; emphasis added)

Once we start reading Scripture through its original Israel-centric lens, God's promises come into sharp focus. But that clarity also brings a challenge. If the Bible is a story that leads to a Messiah, then that Messiah is Israel's from beginning to end. No one replaces God's chosen people. The same God who grafted us in will one day bring the natural branches back to life (Romans 11:25–26). Our place is not to rewrite this story but to receive it with humility, remembering that the promises we share were first made to them.

WHAT IS IMPORTANT TO THE MESSIAH?

We say we love Jesus. We want to be more Christ-like, Messiah-like. We want to love what he loved. So let's slow down and test how deeply we believe that.

When was the last time you read God's promises to Abraham and let them stand as written—without reinterpreting them for yourself? *God wants to bless me through Jesus.* Did you notice he promised land to Abraham's descendants? Or that he pledged to Moses he would dwell among Israel forever and make them a kingdom of priests? Did you assume that by "Israel," God really meant "Christians" (like I did for years)?

Consider God's promise to David. God didn't promise that a man named Jesus would rule invisibly in our hearts from heaven. The promise was that a Jewish descendant of David would one day rule the nations from a throne in Jerusalem forever. Scan the Prophets for mentions of Israel, the twelve tribes, Jerusalem, or Zion. The pages overflow. The land and people of Israel dominate their message. When Jesus said he came "for the lost sheep of the house of Israel," do we think he meant it? It's easy to soften his words, assuming they mean something broader or more symbolic, or convince ourselves that Israel was simply confused about who he really was.

When Paul quotes Isaiah, "A redeemer will come from Zion, and he will remove sins from Jacob," did we picture a Jewish Messiah coming to Jerusalem to cleanse his nation, the very act through which the nations would be blessed? Or did we shrink it to a story about what a personal savior does for us?

When Paul says salvation is "first for the Jew, then for the Greek," do we actually live as if that's true? When Peter calls his audience "the elect and chosen," do we ask who Peter thought the elect and chosen were? Or when John envisions 144,000 from the twelve tribes, do we see a tribal, ethnic Israel—or do we recast it into something else?

All these questions bring us back to the heart of the matter: what do we really believe is important to the Messiah? Our love for Jesus is genuine, but our assumptions often create a Christianized version of him, in place of Israel's Messiah. Questions like these expose how often our default reading of Scripture starts at the end of the story, reading Christianity back into the text rather than letting the story unfold the way the writers themselves first told it. If we love Jesus and want to love what he loves, then we must accept that what he loves may push against the theology we've inherited and the way we've viewed him.

THE CHRISTIAN-CENTRIC LENS OF REPLACEMENT THEOLOGY

Many of us inherited certain assumptions about Israel and the church by osmosis. Few of us were ever *taught* to despise Israel, yet much of Christian tradition has centered itself around a different story. Over time, our theology became more Christian-centric than Israel-centric. At the core, most of us have learned to read Scripture through that lens rather than the one Jesus knew. But to love Jesus well and to read Scriptures as he did, we must acknowledge the reality: the vast majority of Christian theology today emerges from a Replacement Theology, or *supersessionist,* framework.

For many, "Replacement Theology" simply means "the church has replaced Israel." But that's only one piece of the puzzle. (I address the variety of these views more fully in the appendix.) In reality, this paradigm touches nearly every corner of our faith. Replacement Theology assumes that:

- Christians have replaced the Jewish people as heirs to the promises of God

- Grace has replaced the Torah

- Individual believers have replaced the temple

- Jesus has replaced the Levitical priesthood

- Either the church or Jesus himself has replaced national Israel

- Jesus has erased the need for distinct ethnic roles in God's plan

- Salvation/eternal life in heaven has replaced the everlasting Jewish kingdom promised to Abraham and David

Any theology that strips Israel of her ongoing calling or denies her future restoration is, in essence, theft. It robs Israel of the blessings God promised her and hands them to someone else—or declares them void altogether. Worse, it robs the Messiah of his inherently Jewish role. Think about it.

If Christians have replaced the Jewish people as heirs of God's promises …

if grace has made Torah obsolete …

if Jesus has abolished the priesthood, the Temple, and the sacrificial system …

and if national, ethnic Israel no longer matters to God …

… then why do the first half-million words of the Bible revolve around humanity's need for a Jewish Messiah?[12] Why does Matthew open the New Testament by stressing that Jesus is "the son of David, the son of Abraham"? Why does Paul, decades after meeting the risen Jesus, warn Gentiles not to forget the Jewish root that supports them (Romans 11:18)? If the covenant that God swore can be so easily reassigned or dissolved, then what does that say about the God who made it?

Replacement Theology is not inherently malicious. Most of us are simply reading the Bible through the Christian-centric lens of our upbringing. I did this for years. I overlooked the Torah-centered, prophetic portrait of the Messiah in favor of a personal, spiritualized "Christ" because I didn't know any better. But this lens that places Christians at the center has left many of us completely unable to grasp Leviticus, the Jewishness of Jesus, and God's promises to the Jewish people. Because we so rarely approach Scripture through its Israel-centric lens, we have often unintentionally replaced Jewish Israel with Protestant American Christianity at nearly every level. The assumption that Christians are the center of the biblical story has led the church to take a historically low view of the Torah, the Jewish people, the Jewish Messiah, Jewish worship, and perhaps most tragically, the God of the Jews.

These themes run deep in Leviticus, which is one reason so many Christians struggle to understand it. The book can feel dry and tedious at times, but the bigger issue isn't that it's boring—it's that our framework simply isn't strong enough to hold what Leviticus presents. The hard truth is that God chose a family line to bless the nations: the family of Abraham, Israel, led by the Messiah. But his choice was never meant to exclude the rest—it was for the rest. Out of the chosen line flows blessing to the nations, adopting them as sons and daughters, drawing them near to the Father, and making them full heirs in his family. This is a core gospel truth, present from Genesis onward. Through Israel's Messiah, all nations will be blessed.

When I say this, believers light up. We love hearing that, because through faith in Jesus the promises of God belong to us. But there's often an undercurrent of possession, as if these blessings belong more to us than to the Jewish people. For years, I struggled to accept that the gifts, blessings, and future hope that transformed my life did not originate with me.

So few Christians have been prepared to hear the Good News behind these words. God's promises belong first and irrevocably to Israel—and this is not a threat to us. The Jewishness of Jesus ensures God will keep his promises. Through him, the Messiah of Israel, salvation flows to all nations.

> They are Israelites, and to them belong the adoption, the glory, the covenants, the giving of the law, the worship, and the promises. From their race … is the Messiah, who is God over all, blessed forever. Amen. (Romans 9:4–5)

As regards the gospel, [the Jewish people] are enemies for your sake. But as regards election, they are beloved for the sake of their forefathers. For the gifts and the calling of God are irrevocable. (Romans 11:28–29)

Replacement Theology has led many who love Jesus to miss this truth: the Messiah isn't a Christian. He's Jewish, and his mission is inseparable from Israel. To love Jesus and submit to his authority includes caring about what matters to him: the people and land of Israel. "Truly I tell you, whatever you did for one of the least of these brothers and sisters of mine, you did for me" (Matthew 25:40).

THE REAL-WORLD COST OF REPLACEMENT THEOLOGY

This tension isn't just a theoretical one. It shows up in real conversations between Jews and Christians today. Sophiee Suguy is a Jewish blogger who writes on the platform "Judaism is not Christianity Minus Jesus."[13] She explains to her audience the differences between Christianity and Judaism. I have learned a tremendous amount from her work. What strikes me most is how clearly she grasps Christian doctrine and theology, sometimes better than many Christians. In many of her posts, she offers sharp but fair critiques of the way Christians often handle the Hebrew Scriptures. Suguy demonstrates how Christians reassign positive prophecies about Israel to Christians and negative ones to Jews.

For example, Isaiah 49:6: "'I will also make you a light for the nations, that My salvation may reach to the ends of the earth.'" In Jewish context, Suguy shares this refers to Israel's calling to model ethical monotheism. In Christian interpretations, it's often applied to Jesus or the church instead being God's gift to the world. She notes that the opposite happens with negative passages. Verses like Isaiah 1:4, "Woe to the sinful nation, a people whose guilt is great …" are applied literally to the Jewish people as evidence of their failure and rejection of Jesus.

Meanwhile, promises like Jeremiah 31:31–32 of a "new covenant" are reinterpreted to mean that God has moved on from Israel entirely, replacing them with the church. Suguy rightly points out this approach is not only inconsistent in its interpretive strategy, but also reflects theological biases and assumptions. It rewrites Jewish identity and history, ignoring the plain meaning of the texts in their historical and cultural context.

It's no wonder that someone like Sophiee Suguy objects so strongly to the typical Christian portrayal of Jesus and cannot see him as the Messiah her Scriptures point toward. Christianity has not embraced the Jewish Messiah revealed in books like Leviticus.

We can give this framework different names and spins, but at its core, most Christian teaching assumes the same things: Christians are God's people, the church is the primary vehicle for blessing the world, Christ's mission was essentially completed at the resurrection and ascension, and salvation depends on a personal confession of him. None of these are flat-out wrong, but they are not the story of the Torah and the Prophets. Within this system, the restoration of Israel, God's enduring promises to the Jewish people, the earthly reign of the Jewish Messiah, and his plans for the nations are minimized or completely ignored.

These themes, central to nearly every biblical author and vital to practicing Jews today, are stripped of significance. Replacement Theology distances the Jewish people—and, I would argue, Christians themselves—from the gospel, and from truly understanding and loving the people and city our God has inscribed on the palms of his hands. Sadly, Christianity has not preached a gospel "first to the Jew." We have preached it first to ourselves.

FINAL THOUGHTS

This book is not just about Leviticus. It's about how we perceive it—and how leaving it out of our faith costs us knowing who Jesus really is, what he came to do, and the gospel he preached.

Up to this point, we've looked at the lenses we bring to the Bible: Christian-centric assumptions leave us with an anemic Torah and a story stripped of its Jewish Messiah. For years my faith operated within this framework, and it's why Leviticus never mattered to me. I read it backward, forcing onto the text what I thought I already knew about Jesus, the temple, and the priesthood. In doing so, I killed Leviticus, robbing myself and others of the gospel it preaches.

Recovering Leviticus—and with it, the Messiah and what he loves—hasn't been easy. Questioning long-held assumptions forces us to face uncomfortable truths most of us would rather avoid. But hard questions are the engine of real faith. They drive us deeper into the living Word and reveal our need for a Messiah in the first place.

Too often, though, we never ask the hard questions about Leviticus. We've already made up our minds: Jesus "fulfilled it," so it's finished. Conversation over. But if there's no more need for Leviticus, then there's no more need for the Jewish people. And if the Jewish people don't matter, then we're back to reading the Bible as an Evangelical story about us and God alone—our forgiveness, our salvation. That story has no need for a Jewish Messiah, Israel, or the Torah—and no reason to read Leviticus.

Our Christian-centric reading is not robust enough to carry the weight of Leviticus. So we mostly leave it out of the story—and when we do bring it in, we twist it to fit our conclusions. We stretch its meaning through a kind of scriptural gymnastics, reshaping Leviticus to serve a later, Christian-centric framework that ends up cutting us off from the gospel of Leviticus and its Jewish Messiah.

Jesus didn't do that. Neither did any other biblical author. They didn't bend Scripture to fit their worldview. They humbled themselves to submit to the worldview Scripture gave them. We can do the same. We can recover a better foundation. We can learn to love Jesus as the Messiah he says he is, and understand his role—and ours—within Israel's story. Leviticus is vital to that story. If we are willing to take it seriously, we can finally see why it matters to him—and why it should matter to us.

From here, we'll focus on understanding how Jesus does not replace Leviticus—and why that matters. But this isn't simply a new way of forcing Leviticus into categories we've inherited. It means honoring its place as the heart of the Torah and letting it confront our assumptions by harmonizing with the rest of Scripture. Ahead, we'll ask: when Jesus said he came to fulfill the Torah, what did he mean? How do the Prophets, the first believers, the apostles, and the Letter to the Hebrews understand Leviticus? We must learn to situate our view of Leviticus within the framework that the biblical authors used.

Doing this will raise a lot of questions. For many, the lens of Replacement Theology is all we've ever known. So along the way, I try to offer biblically grounded responses—sometimes different from traditional explanations. That's okay. In a culture that is quick to take offense, we need to recover the art of honest conversation, especially when it means questioning familiar beliefs.

If you are willing to take on this challenge, I invite you to open the passages I refer to for yourself. Step into the theater of Scripture and wrestle with God. It's demanding, sometimes uncomfortable work, but he is a gracious partner and a fair match. Like Jacob, those who wrestle come away changed—blessed and renamed, carrying a faith shaped not by culture, family, or traditions, but by the God who made us and calls us into his plans. Scripture doesn't change. God doesn't change. But we do.

Deep within my heart I believe there is a more authentic way to understand this book that lies forgotten and lifeless within our hands. One that draws us nearer to God and restores its voice within the Good News he wants us to hear. Leviticus mattered to the Messiah—and if we want to follow him faithfully, we cannot afford to ignore it.

5

JESUS ON LEVITICUS

IF YOU'VE BEEN IN CHURCH LONG ENOUGH, you have probably heard it said that Jesus came to free us from the law. The Torah carries a reputation for being burdensome, outdated, and for someone else. The gospel, in this telling, is the relief of being done with all that "Old Testament stuff." We assume that the law—and all it entails—is replaced by Jesus.

But Jesus says something that doesn't fit neatly into that narrative. Let's start here, with his own words. Whatever our theology says, we love Jesus and want to follow him better. That's ground we can all stand on. So what did he actually say about the Torah, and by extension, Leviticus?

JESUS'S CLAIMS ABOUT THE TORAH

One of Jesus's most famous statements about Leviticus comes from the Sermon on the Mount:

> Do not think that I have come to abolish the Torah or the Prophets; I have not come to abolish them but to fill them to the fullest. For truly, I say to you, until heaven and earth pass away, not an iota, not a dot, will pass from the Torah until all is accomplished. Therefore whoever relaxes one of the least of these commandments and teaches others to do the same will be called least in the kingdom of heaven, but whoever does them and teaches them will be called great in the kingdom of heaven. (Matthew 5:17–19)

In this passage, Jesus makes four distinct statements:

1. What he is not doing: He did not abolish the Torah or the Prophets.

2. What he is doing: He is fulfilling them.

3. A timeframe for completing the work: The Torah stands until heaven and earth pass away.

4. A final, stern warning: Relaxing the Torah will be costly in the kingdom.

Let's take a closer look at his first three claims.

Claim #1: Jesus Is Not Abolishing the Torah

In the passage, the word translated "abolish" (*katalyō*) means to tear something down, dismantle it, or make it useless—like demolishing a building so it no longer stands. In essence he says, *"Don't imagine I've come to dismantle or invalidate the Torah and the Prophets. That's not my mission."*

Claim #2: Jesus Is Fulfilling the Torah

Instead, Jesus says he fills them to the fullest. The word "fulfill" used here (*plēroō*) means to fill something to the top, or to bring it to its intended completeness with nothing lacking. Imagine a glass not just topped off at the brim, but overflowing with water. This is what Jesus promises to do with the Torah and the Prophets. He isn't replacing them with himself; he's bringing them to life in their fullest form. In doing so, he follows the line of the Hebrew prophets who longed for the day when God would give his people a new heart and a new covenant—so they could finally live out the laws he gave them. *"I'm not here to bulldoze the house; I'm here to finish it so it can be everything it was meant to be."*

Claim #3: Jesus Has a Timeframe in Mind for Fulfilling the Torah

Jesus's third claim in this statement tells us when and how he plans to bring this "fulfilling" about. He says that every part of the Torah will remain in effect "until heaven and earth pass away." In other words, he connects its authority to the lifespan of the current world. By anchoring the Torah's authority to the endurance of heaven and earth, Jesus is saying that its validity lasts as long as the world itself lasts. Only when this creation is remade will all that the Torah and Prophets teach be brought to their final completion. Jesus did not envision the Torah being completed during his lifetime, nor at his death or resurrection. For him, its destiny continues, rooted in the enduring word of God, which will outlast even creation itself.

As Jesus shared this vision with his Jewish audience, they would have understood exactly what he meant. They too believed the Torah would endure as long as creation itself.[14] And as he continues in the rest of the Sermon on the Mount, Jesus expands the Torah's wisdom, showing that it remains—and will always remain—the standard for God's people and his Kingdom.

If that's true, then the story he tells about the Torah's endurance points forward, not backward, toward a future still unfolding. This means that the Messiah's mission isn't over yet. Jesus saw the Torah's fulfillment carrying well beyond the cross. His task was bigger than the moment of his death. Yet this part of the story is one that Christian tradition rarely tells. Because the Messiah's coming reign is underdeveloped in Christian teaching, we've explained Jesus's words in ways that fit our traditions but don't precisely fit his own words.

In the Protestant retelling, Jesus fulfilled the Torah with his own life and personal obedience, bringing the law to its fullest meaning. We imagine that he expanded its commands, teaching us their intended purpose. "Don't murder" really means "Don't even get angry." And this expansion is what it means for Jesus to fulfill the Torah. Or we picture the cross as a turning point where Torah was fulfilled and traded out for something "better": Jesus himself and his teaching, leaving us to simply follow the "Law of Christ." In that version, Torah is just a placeholder, meant to reveal sin, but now it has no further value. Our obedience isn't to God's Torah anymore, but to Jesus.

While Jesus certainly expanded on the Torah and illuminated its wisdom, this is only a small part of what he thought it meant for the Torah and Prophets to reach their fullness. Jesus's vision of the Torah goes much further than we usually give him credit for. That's why he said it would be easier for heaven and earth to vanish than for even the smallest command of the Torah to lose its purpose (Luke 16:17). He never implies he has something better than the Torah to offer or that its commands lose authority because he revealed their true nature. And he never implies that the Torah is something that expired with his coming. Yet this is the dominant way the church treats it: Jesus "set us free from the law," so the sacrifices, purity laws, festivals, and temple worship of Leviticus all vanish at the cross.

That's inconsistent with what Jesus says. He saw Torah's future woven right into the story it tells. All through his ministry, he taught and expounded on its commands, insisting on its lasting authority. In his story, the Messiah's job is to make sure the Torah and Prophets reach their intended goal. But in the Evangelical version, Jesus came mainly to forgive sin, save us from judgment, and secure us a spot in heaven—his work essentially finished at the cross and resurrection.

If that's our picture, we'll never make sense of what Jesus actually says here. Because in Scripture's portrait, the Messiah's work doesn't end with an empty tomb. It points to a reign of justice and peace still to come. His first coming began Torah's fulfillment, and the resurrection is proof that God will finish what he started. But the story isn't over yet. Messiah still has more to do.

Claim #4: Jesus's Final Warning

Jesus knew exactly how the Torah fit into the work still ahead, and he doesn't soften his stance. He backs it up with a sobering warning: "Therefore whoever relaxes one of the least of these commandments and teaches others to do the same will be called least in the kingdom of heaven, but whoever does them and teaches them will be called great in the kingdom of heaven."

Far from saying, *"You don't have to worry about Torah obedience anymore because I made it simpler. I'm fulfilling the Torah by obedient for you,"* Jesus declares the opposite. Dismissing even the smallest command, or teaching others to, diminishes one's standing in the kingdom. Why? Because Torah has a role in what is still to come. For him, Torah is part of the kingdom, both now and eschatologically. It's not optional. Its authority, down to the smallest detail, remains binding, beautiful, and necessary until the day God's plan is complete.

JESUS LIVED LEVITICUS AND THE PRACTICED THE TORAH HE TAUGHT

Jesus didn't just defend the Torah with words. He actively lived it. He was a Torah-observant Jew who practiced Leviticus. His life and ministry demonstrate that he saw no contradiction between his mission as Messiah and obedience to the commands God gave through the Torah, including those in Leviticus.

1. He was raised in the Levitical tradition.
From the very beginning, Jesus was raised in accordance with Levitical tradition. His parents circumcised him on the eighth day (Luke 2:21) as commanded in Leviticus 12:3, and Mary fulfilled the purification rites after childbirth by offering the sacrifices prescribed in Leviticus 12:6–8 (Luke 2:22–24). These early acts by his devoted Jewish parents grounded Jesus in the patterns and precepts of the Torah from infancy.

2. He kept the sacred calendar.
Jesus's life followed the sacred calendar God gave Israel. He traveled to Jerusalem for Passover (Luke 2:41–42; John 2:13, 12:1,12), celebrated Sukkot—the Feast of Tabernacles (John 7:2, 10, 14), and even took part in Hanukkah, the Feast of Dedication (John 10:22–23). These weren't just cultural customs that Jesus begrudgingly participated in. They were acts of worship and heartfelt expressions of loyalty to the God of Israel. He even looked forward to celebrating Passover *again* in the future in the Kingdom of God (Luke 22:15–16).

3. He honored the purity laws.
Jesus instructed those he healed to follow the Levitical purity procedures. For example, he told the cleansed leper to "show yourself to the priest and offer the gift Moses commanded" (Matthew 8:4; see Leviticus 14). These are not the words of a man who saw the requirement as outmoded. Despite the fact that he personally healed the man, Jesus believed Leviticus provided important boundaries to keep God's house pure in Jerusalem.

4. He upheld the sacrificial system.
Jesus recognized the validity of the sacrificial offerings. He affirmed

that the altar sanctifies the gift (Matthew 23:18–20) and that offerings were to be brought in reconciliation (Matthew 5:23–24), showing he still saw the temple service as an outworking of proper worship as well as life in community with others.

5. *He practiced and taught love as Leviticus defines it.*

When asked about the greatest commandments, Jesus brought together two central Torah passages—Leviticus 19:18, "Love your neighbor as yourself" (requoted in Matthew 22:39), and the Shema from Deuteronomy 6:4–5, the call to love God with all one's heart, soul, and strength. This pairing is profound. It unites love for God and love for others as the inseparable foundation of the Torah. The Shema remains central to Jewish prayer and worship today, and for Jesus, these two commands summed up the heart of God's instruction. His teachings, healings, and compassion toward the marginalized were living demonstrations of this Levitical command in action.

6. *He respected the priesthood and honored temple service.*

Jesus taught in the temple courts (John 7:14, Luke 19:47) and acknowledged the authority of the priests in their role as teachers of the Torah (Matthew 23:2–3), even when he rebuked their hypocrisy. He also defended the sanctity of the temple itself, driving out those who turned it into a marketplace (Matthew 21:12–13, John 2:13–17). From his childhood, Jesus was deeply drawn to the temple, sitting among its teachers, listening and asking questions (Luke 2:41–49). For Jesus, the temple was the House of Yahweh on earth, a vital place of intimate connection between God and his people.

7. *He honored the Sabbath as holy.*

Jesus observed the Jewish shabbat (sundown Friday to sundown Saturday), joining his fellow Jews in synagogue gatherings for worship and teaching (Luke 4:16, Mark 1:21). While he challenged certain human traditions that distorted its purpose, he never dismissed shabbat.

By healing on the Sabbath and teaching in its assemblies, Jesus demonstrated that the day God sanctified at creation and gave to his people in the Torah (Leviticus 23:3) remained a gift for God's people, a sacred space in time for meeting God in his presence.

Jesus practiced Leviticus. He was a Torah-observant Jew who lived out the very commands he taught. He never saw Leviticus in conflict with himself or role as Messiah. The Torah was the central hope and foundation for his message.

THE PROBLEM WITH PICKING AND CHOOSING

These ideas bring us to an important point. Jesus's words and example leave no room for treating the Torah like a buffet, picking and choosing which parts we affirm based on our comfort level or cultural preferences.

When Jesus explained commands like "You shall not murder" or "You shall not commit adultery," he wasn't discarding the old to install something new—he was exposing the heart beneath the command. In every so-called "supersession," Jesus reveals the wisdom of the law by showing what it always meant, not by replacing it with something else. Most Christian traditions readily affirm the creation account, humanity's calling as image bearers, and the Ten Commandments. Yet we treat the Levitical instructions as if they belonged to a different Bible altogether. The Torah, however, does not come to us in disconnected pieces—and neither does Jesus divide it. He shows it to be a single, God-breathed work with a unified purpose, each part supporting and illuminating the others.

That's why, throughout this book, you'll notice me using Leviticus and Torah almost interchangeably. After all, are we really asking whether Jesus replaces Leviticus—or whether he replaces the Torah itself? The two are so intertwined that to speak of one without implying the other is nearly impossible for me as I write.

If we pick and choose from Leviticus (or from any part of the Torah), we pick and choose who Jesus is. We cannot claim him as Savior while disregarding the foundation of his teaching. Leviticus is woven into the same fabric as Genesis, Exodus, Numbers, and Deuteronomy, and pulling out its threads weakens the entire garment. This is why Jesus's words in Matthew 5 are so uncompromising. If we claim to believe him, we cannot affirm parts of the Torah in theory while rejecting its core book in practice. He never said, *"I've come to uphold the Torah—except for the priestly laws, sacrifices, and purity instructions. I'm abolishing all that."* He affirmed all of it—every dot and stroke—until the day heaven and earth are renewed. For him, Leviticus remains essential to God's plan.

That conviction shaped not only his teaching but his practice. Jesus didn't play fast and loose with the Torah. He honored it as a faithful, first-century Jew who lived and breathed its words. What sometimes looks like selective obedience to us was, in fact, a familiar *halachic* approach—applying the Torah's wisdom to changing circumstances. His disagreements with other teachers were not about the Torah's relevance but about the heart behind obedience.[15]

Take Mark 7 as one example. At first glance, it can sound as though Jesus abolished Israel's dietary laws when he said that nothing entering a person from outside can defile them. Many Christian interpretations have taken the editorial note—"thus he declared all foods clean" (7:19)—as a sweeping cancellation of the kosher laws that God gave Israel. But that's not what's happening in the passage.

The dispute isn't about pork or shellfish at all. It begins with the Pharisees questioning Jesus for skipping a ritual handwashing ceremony—a Pharisaic tradition meant to preserve purity before eating. The debate was not whether certain foods were permitted, but whether neglecting that ritual could make a person impure. In the passage, Jesus neither abolishes the food laws nor elevates them beyond their intended purpose. Instead, he draws his listeners back to the wisdom at the heart of purity rituals to begin with: impurity doesn't begin with what enters the mouth but with what emerges from within.

"In declaring all foods clean," Jesus didn't overturn the dietary laws: the text itself never shows this, nor did his Jewish disciples abandon their kosher practice—a controversy that would later arise only as

Gentiles entered the faith. Rather, he rescued their meaning. The food laws were never about mere menu restrictions but about cultivating discernment—a reminder to make distinctions and to bring into one's life only what is acceptable before God. The Pharisees' interpretations of purity had made the laws and rituals so burdensome that they voided God's very purpose.

Jesus exposed how easily the Torah's intent could be obscured by human tradition: "You leave the commandment of God and hold to the tradition of men" (Mark 7:8). He didn't say, "Now that I've explained the principle, you can stop practicing the law." He called people to recover the command's heart—to live its wisdom rather than replace it. The apostles carried that understanding forward. While Jewish believers continued observing the Torah's food laws, Gentiles were welcomed without those same obligations—lest any human restriction distort God's intent to include them and place unnecessary burdens upon them.

Ironically, by claiming that Jesus superseded certain laws of the Torah, many Christians have repeated the very mistake he confronted—honoring human tradition over divine intent. In our eagerness to exalt our own interpretations of texts like these and justify our own traditions, we have often severed the commands from their story and missed their enduring wisdom. Jesus did not treat the Torah as not a list of rules to keep or discard, but a living narrative filled with commands meant to impart understanding. Our task is not to reconstruct an ancient society or dissect it into convenient parts to keep or discard, but to do as Jesus did—to honor what it still says. To look carefully at its wisdom, to discern whether we have embodied it faithfully, and to guard our hearts from the impurity that comes from within. In this, we follow the very spirit of understanding Jesus modeled.

FINAL THOUGHTS

When we listen carefully to Jesus, we hear no whisper of a Torah fulfilled only to be set aside or simplified into some broad definition of basic goodness. Instead, we hear him affirm, emphatically, that it remains weighty and functional today.

Jesus did not come to end the practices outlined in Leviticus, nor to replace the authority of the Torah or the Prophets. He submitted to them, taught them, and instructed his followers to do the same. He believed their meaning, revealing the depth of what they were always pointing toward—God's coming kingdom and his presence dwelling among his people. Later Christian theology would interpret these realities in new ways, but that development belongs to the Church's later history, not to the message Jesus himself preached. He never claimed to supersede the role of the temple or the priesthood, nor did he speak against sacrificial worship at any time. Instead, he trusted their truest purpose, teaching that each command points toward God's promise of renewal. He showed those who already knew these commands how to live them with greater faith and understanding.

Jesus viewed Leviticus, along with the rest of the Torah, as a living, ongoing guide. The same commands that once set ancient Israel apart continue to form the framework for life under Messiah's reign, shaping a holy people who reflect his character to the world. Jesus never envisioned the Torah fulfilled at the moment of his death, resurrection, or coming return. Its value remains ongoing and its teachings authoritative until he has fully accomplished them all.

The question we have not yet answered is: *how did Jesus know this?* In the Sermon on the Mount, he didn't spell out where this information came from. He didn't need to. His audience already knew the Scriptures that formed his identity. Jesus knew the Torah itself testified to the Messiah's mission. But the Prophets carried that testimony further. Their oracles sharpened the outlines of what Leviticus already described. Without them, his teaching on the Torah would remain incomplete. With them, the picture of Messiah's mission—fulfilling Levitical worship and carrying it to its goal—comes into full focus.

6

THE PROPHETIC VISION OF LEVITICUS

THE STORY BEHIND JESUS'S CLAIM that he came to fulfill the Torah and the Prophets was not his own invention. He knew it from the Torah and from Israel's Prophets—and so did his audience. But here's the problem: we cannot believe, as Jesus did, "all that the Prophets have spoken" if we don't actually know what the Prophets have spoken.

What did the Prophets have to say about Leviticus? Leviticus gave Israel the patterns of worship; the Prophets showed that those patterns would one day crescendo in the Messiah's reign. When we turn to the prophets—the very ones who gave us some of the most powerful visions of our Messiah—we find a surprising picture. Far from portraying Levitical worship as obsolete, the prophets consistently envision a future in which the temple is central, the priesthood is restored, and the nations are gathered to worship through the rhythms of Torah. In their visions of the Messiah's reign, it is clear that sacrifice, sacred space, and Israel's festivals are not discarded. The Messiah does not "fulfill" the story by canceling Leviticus or replacing it with himself. He oversees it, revitalizes it, and ultimately reigns within its framework.

THE MESSIANIC REIGN

If we want to understand the prophets on their own terms, we need to describe the future the way they do. Many people use the term *millennium* to describe the period in which the Messiah rules on earth. I find the term to be unhelpful. The word *millennium*—drawn solely from the thousand years of Revelation 20—doesn't appear anywhere in Scripture. It's a term that has become deeply entangled in a wide array of theological systems, many of which diverge sharply from the prophetic tradition. *Millennium* often generates more confusion for people, carrying with it modern assumptions and timelines foreign to the prophets.

For that reason, I prefer to call the time when Jesus rules on earth *the messianic reign*. It captures exactly what the Messiah is doing. He's reigning. This term places the emphasis where the prophets do—on the reign of the God's David-like king who dwells with his people, restores justice, and leads Israel and the nations in worship.

For many believers, this picture feels unfamiliar. Christianity doesn't emphasize the messianic reign or imagine eternity through a Jewish lens. But the Messiah ruling from Zion, the temple restored, and Torah flowing to the nations is the world that the prophets actually envisioned. That is the vision we want to stay anchored to as we move forward. Their words give us a clear window into what the reign of the Messiah will look like, if we are willing to step into their world and see through their eyes. When we do, we find that his reign is profoundly Levitical.

The restored temple, the active priesthood, the appointed feasts, and the sacrificial system all stand at the heart of his rule.[16]

THE PROPHETS AND LEVITICAL WORSHIP IN THE AGE TO COME

To see this for ourselves, let's step into the world of some of the prophets—Isaiah, Zechariah, Jeremiah, and Ezekiel—whose visions give us some of the clearest portraits of the messianic reign in the Hebrew Scriptures.

Isaiah: Zion as the Center

Isaiah is a natural starting point, offering sweeping prophecies that set the tone for the messianic age. His scroll opens with a vision where the restored temple, altar, and Torah stand at the heart of creation itself. In Isaiah 2:2–3, the "mountain of the house of the LORD" is lifted above every other height, and people from many nations say to one another: "Come, let us go up to the mountain of the LORD, to the house of the God of Jacob, that he may teach us his ways and that we may walk in his paths. "For out of Zion shall go the law, and the word of the LORD from Jerusalem."

There's no mistaking Isaiah's point: the nations are drawn to Zion to worship Yahweh and learn Torah. It's here at God's house—the temple—that they receive his specific righteous standards. Leviticus is not sidelined. Isaiah depicts Jerusalem as a place with an altar, where sacrifices and gifts are offered to Yahweh in great joy: "All the flocks of Kedar shall be gathered to you; the rams of Nebaioth shall minister to you; they shall come up with acceptance on my altar, and I will beautify my beautiful house" (Isaiah 60:7). "They shall call you the City of the LORD, the Zion of the Holy One of Israel" (Isaiah 60:14).

In Isaiah's imagination, the streets of Jerusalem come alive with worshippers, nations streaming in with gifts, smoke rising from the altar, and songs of joy echoing from the temple courts. To this picture Isaiah returns again and again: Zion as the world's spiritual center, the temple as a place of joy and worship, and the Torah as the enduring expression of God's will—not just for Israel, but for all nations.

Zechariah: Nations at the Feast

Zechariah picks up the same themes as Isaiah: "Thus says the LORD: I have returned to Zion and will dwell in the midst of Jerusalem, and Jerusalem shall be called the faithful city, and the mountain of the LORD of hosts, the holy mountain" (Zechariah 8:3). Here too, Yahweh's return signals that His holy space—a space protected and maintained by Levitical rituals—has been reestablished. The prophetic vision hits a crescendo in Zechariah 14, where the nations go up to Jerusalem "year after year to worship the King, the LORD of hosts, and to keep the Feast of Booths" (Zechariah 14:16). Picture nations leaving their national holidays behind and streaming up to Jerusalem, building booths in the streets, celebrating the Feast of Tabernacles together. Zechariah envisions a world reoriented around Leviticus. Even Gentiles participate in Israel's liturgical calendar. The Feast of Tabernacles (one of the pilgrimage feasts outlined in Leviticus 23) is not set aside but celebrated by people from all over the world. Holiness saturates everything, from temple vessels to the bells on horses (Zechariah 14:20–21). Zechariah draws heavily on categories from Leviticus—sacred space, sacred time, sacred things. These things aren't obsolete during the messianic reign. They expand beyond Israel's borders to reshape the world.

Jeremiah: The Branch and the Priests

This same thread also runs through Jeremiah's prophecies. Often remembered for his laments, Jeremiah also speaks with striking hope about the days to come. In Jeremiah 33:14–18, he promises that God will raise up a righteous Branch from David's line who will execute justice and righteousness in the land. In that same passage, God declares that the Levitical priesthood will never lack a man to stand before him to offer burnt offerings, grain offerings, and sacrifices continually. The restored Davidic throne and Levitical service stand side by side, inseparable in Jeremiah's portrait of the age to come. For him, covenant renewal is not just about law written on hearts but also about worship offered at the altar in God's house.

Ezekiel: The Shepherd and the Sanctuary

Ezekiel takes this vision the farthest. From chapters 34 to 48, he sketches a sweeping picture of restoration: Israel renewed, the nations judged, evil purged, and the entire human family brought into alignment with God's standards. At the heart of it all is a figure Ezekiel calls God's Shepherd—a royal servant from David's line: "I will set up over them one shepherd, my servant David, and he shall feed them … I the LORD will be their God, and my servant David shall be prince among them" (Ezekiel 34:23–24). This Shepherd-King doesn't rule from a distance. He lives among his people, leading with justice and guiding them in covenant faithfulness: "My servant David shall be king over them … and they shall walk in my rules and be careful to obey my statutes" (Ezekiel 37:24).

Ezekiel was a priest, and it shows. He envisions the messianic reign as a time marked by worship, obedience, and the abiding presence of God's sanctuary among His people: "My dwelling place shall be with them, and I will be their God, and they shall be my people" (Ezekiel 37:27). In chapters 40–48, he presents a detailed vision of a renewed temple—grand in scale, saturated with holiness, and filled with order. There is a faithful Levitical priesthood, serving in purity. Sacrifices are offered, the sacred calendar is honored, and the Feast of Tabernacles is joyfully kept. But my favorite part of this vision is Ezekiel's description of the river (Ezekiel 47).

Picture yourself at the temple's threshold, where a trickle of water seeps from beneath the foundation stones. Step by step it swells—ankle-deep, knee-deep, waist-deep—until it surges into a mighty river. It rushes through the wilderness, turning barren deserts into gardens and filling lifeless seas with teeming fish. It's Eden overflowing to all creation, starting right there at the temple. In Ezekiel's vision, the restoration of Levitical worship under the messianic shepherd-king is the very way God begins to heal the world.

Together, these prophets sing in harmony—a prophetic chorus announcing the age when the Davidic king rules from Jerusalem, the Levitical priesthood serves in purity, and the nations joyfully join Israel in worshipping Yahweh according to his Torah. These are all themes that find their roots and language in Leviticus.

LEVITICAL WORSHIP IN THE MINOR PROPHETS

The longer prophetic books give us sweeping visions, but the so-called Minor Prophets—twelve shorter scrolls spanning centuries of Israel's life—add vivid detail. At first glance, their sharp condemnations of Israel's worship might sound like rejections of the whole Levitical system. But that's not what's happening. Their rebukes target Israel's corruption of it, not the framework itself. What they longed for was not Leviticus's removal, but its renewal. They hope for a day when worship to God is given as he intended.

Amos and Micah: Justice as Worship

Take Amos and Micah. Both deliver scathing critiques of temple rituals divorced from justice. Amos thunders, "I hate, I reject your festivals … But let justice roll down like waters" (Amos 5:21,24). Imagine the streets of northern Israel buzzing with festival crowds—musicians playing, priests chanting, worshippers lining up with offerings. Into that noise steps Amos, his words cutting through like a thunderclap: God doesn't despise the feasts themselves, but the hypocrisy of hands lifted in worship while the poor are trampled in the marketplace.

Micah paints the scene differently, like a courtroom drama. Israel stands before the Judge, clutching sacrifices and asking nervously, "With what shall I come before the LORD? Thousands of rams? Rivers of oil?" The answer shocks them. God doesn't want bribes of blood or oil without changed hearts. He wants justice, mercy, humility.

These prophets are not abandoning Levitical categories but defending their true purpose. Leviticus 19, often overlooked, holds holiness and justice together—sacrificial worship bound inseparably with neighborly love. Amos and Micah demand not less Levitical worship, but more of it as God intended. Their prophetic call never pointed toward another people revising Israel's worship, but toward restoring its heart *within* Israel. Later generations—including the earliest followers of Jesus—would wrestle with how to live that vision out (the topic of another chapter). But the prophets' concern was clear: not transformed practices of faith, but renewed covenant faithfulness.

Haggai and Malachi: Restoring God's House

After the exile, Haggai urges the people to rebuild the temple, not for national pride, but because the sanctuary is essential for covenant life. He even appeals to the priests using Levitical purity laws (Haggai 2:11–14), affirming that temple service must meet God's standards of holiness. Malachi is perhaps the most direct of the minor prophets in affirming the enduring nature of Levitical worship. God declares that the "covenant with Levi" remains intact (Malachi 2:4–5), and that he will return to his temple to purify the priesthood so that offerings can once again be made in righteousness (Malachi 3:1–4). Far from canceling the sacrificial system, Malachi anticipates its refinement and future restoration.

Across these scrolls, the themes of sacrifice, priesthood, holiness, and sacred time are never dismissed. When the prophets critique Israel's worship, they weren't tearing Leviticus down—they were calling for its rescue. They envision a day when Messiah reigns, and worship is finally what it was meant to be—spirit and truth expressed through renewed Levitical life.

THE PROPHETIC USE OF LEVITICAL CATEGORIES

All these prophetic visions we've explored are saturated with Levitical vocabulary and themes. Holiness, purity, sacrifice, sacred space, sacred time—these are concepts that the prophets inherited from Leviticus. These categories gave them language to call Israel back into faithfulness and provided the framework for envisioning a restored world. Leviticus is how God could dwell among his people, and the prophets simply cannot imagine a future in which these practices are no more.

This is where many of us start squirming. Animal sacrifices? Levite priests? In a future kingdom? We rush to find workarounds—maybe they're just symbols, maybe they're only memorials—anything to make them less … bloody. But whatever our explanations, they don't change what the prophets foresaw.

It's sometimes suggested that the prophets meant something deeper or symbolic—that they were really pointing ahead to Christ's future sacrifice or to a spiritualized kind of worship. But that would have been foreign to their world. These weren't mystics inventing metaphors; they were Israelites speaking within Israel's story. Their visions of temple, priesthood, and sacrifice flowed from the only worship they knew—worship centered in Leviticus.

To read them otherwise is not a small interpretive shift. It imposes later understandings on an ancient worldview, as though their meaning could only find its truest completion once Christian theology arrived. That's a remarkably high view of ourselves—and a low one of them. It assumes that the prophets, and even the generations of Jewish interpreters after them (including those who confessed Jesus as Messiah), somehow misunderstood their own Scriptures until the church came along to clarify them.

In conversations like these, we need to ask whether that is really the most responsible—and the most loving—way to engage our prophetic neighbors. The Christian suggestion isn't invalid, but it is later, and it reflects a world far removed from the one in which the prophets spoke and the visions Jesus affirmed.

This also raises the familiar question almost everyone asks about the prophets: should we take these visions literally or symbolically? That's the wrong question. A better one is, "What does it mean?" The prophets weren't drawing modern lines between literal and symbolic. They were describing what God revealed to them while standing in the cultural river they knew, its banks and currents shaping how they spoke to their audience. To understand them sympathetically, we have to ask what their visions meant to the people who first heard them.

For those original audiences, the message was unmistakable: when the Messiah reigns, the world will be ordered around the same sacred order that once ordered Israel—temple, priesthood, feast, and sacrifice. Whether every detail was literal or representative was not their concern; what was clear to them was that Levitical worship endures alongside the Messiah's rule. That expectation may trouble modern readers, but it didn't trouble them.

In fact, their confidence is even more striking when we remember the timing. Many of these prophecies came when such worship was impossible. Much of Israel's prophetic literature was written during or after the exile. The temple lay in ruins, its courts defiled and silent, its altar cold. Yet, the very things Israel had lost became the centerpiece of the prophets' hope. Ezekiel, especially, shows how essential Levitical worship was to his vision of renewal. For him, a new covenant without a restored sanctuary was inconceivable. The rebuilding of sacred space, the reestablishment of a faithful priesthood, the return of ordered sacrifice—this was God's heart for Israel's future.

That future wasn't just for Israel alone. The prophets foresaw a day when the Gentile nations would not simply watch Levitical worship from a distance, but take part in it. Isaiah is explicit: "The foreigners who join themselves to the LORD ... these I will bring to my holy mountain, and make them joyful in my house of prayer ... for my house shall be called a house of prayer for all peoples" (Isaiah 56:6–7). In this vision, the sacred space of Leviticus isn't diminished to include the nations. It's expanded. Its categories—sacrifice, Sabbath, priesthood, purity—become the shared language of worship for the human family, carried forward from the same river that shaped Israel's life with God.

For modern Gentile believers, this changes the frame entirely. It echoes precisely what Jesus affirmed in Matthew. The prophetic hope is not that we would be freed from Torah, but drawn into it. The prophets welcomed Gentiles into the rhythms of covenant life with the God of Israel.

FINAL THOUGHTS

The messianic reign is one of those powerful threads running through

Scripture that keeps calling me back—urging me to lay aside assumptions and let the Spirit open my eyes to what's always been there. The more I return to the Prophets, the more I realize how easily we can read past their visions without really seeing them—especially when it comes to how they imagined the age to come. We can, of course, read the Prophets however we want. Or like Leviticus, we can avoid reading them at all. That's the problem.

It's easy to reconstruct their visions to fit our existing categories, to remold their words into images of our own making. We each bring our own frameworks and experiences—that's not wrong; it's simply human. The challenge is to recognize those lenses and set them aside long enough to hear the Prophets in their own voices, to see Leviticus through their eyes instead of ours. When we don't, we start reshaping their message, softening what they describe or reinterpreting their temple visions through a lens that feels more familiar to us simply because we see the world differently. But in doing so, we risk missing what they actually show: a Jewish Messiah reigning in a Jewish way, among a faithful people practicing Levitical worship. This was, candidly, their hope.

Sometimes I wonder what Jesus felt when he stood on that hillside, preaching the most famous sermon the world has ever known. I imagine him looking out over the crowds—the poor in spirit, the mourners, the meek, the hungry—dust on their feet, weariness in their eyes, the weight of life pressing down on their daily lives. These people knew more about loss than abundance, more about oppression than freedom. But maybe he didn't see just their present struggle. Maybe on that dusty hillside he could see the vision of Isaiah, Zechariah, and Ezekiel coming alive: the last becoming first, the weary clothed in gladness, nations streaming to Zion, all humanity worshipping in joy. Maybe he saw a world healed and reordered, with those very people—bruised, ignored, powerless—now swept into the life-giving river flowing from the temple, gathered around him in a restored Jerusalem, carried by its current into the life of the Creator. I don't think he called them blessed only because the teachings of the Torah could live in their hearts that very day. I think he called them blessed because he knew that one day the Torah would be the air they breathed—and he was the one chosen to make it so. Leviticus was part of that order, bringing the blessings the prophets foretold.

This vision may unsettle modern readers. The idea of animal sacrifice or Levitical ritual in the age to come raises hard questions. But the discomfort is ours—not the prophets', and not Jesus's. For them, the harmony of the Messiah and Leviticus wasn't a problem. It was the kingdom. And it's the kingdom we are invited to expect too. To long for this kingdom is to long for the world the prophets saw—a world where Messiah reigns, Leviticus sings, and the nations breathe the air of Torah.

7

THE FAITH OF THE FIRST BELIEVERS

IT'S ONE THING TO HEAR THE PROPHETS SPEAK across the centuries; it's another to watch how the men and women who knew Jesus lived after he was gone. Their choices, their worship, and their teaching give us a living answer to the question: does Leviticus still matter? If it was meant to fade away, surely those who walked with him would have been the first to know. In the decades after his ascension, how did Jesus's closest followers view the Torah's place in their lives? The book of Acts gives us the answer.

Acts doesn't describe Christianity's birth. It shows Judaism's continuation. Acts portrays Jesus's first followers as Jews who continued practicing Judaism just as they always had. When they came to believe that Jesus was the Messiah, they didn't "become Christians" and break away from Judaism to start something new. They remained Sabbath-keeping, Torah-observant, son-circumcising, feast-celebrating, sacrifice-offering, temple-gathering Jews.[17] Even many of the Levite priests came to confess Jesus as Messiah (Acts 6:7) and kept right on with their priestly duties.

The first time I really noticed that detail, it stopped me in my tracks. I had read Acts dozens of times, yet somehow completely missed the fact that when these priests confessed Jesus, they didn't hand in their two-week notice the next day! They still showed up for the morning sacrifice, still taught the people God's instructions, still sang the psalms appointed for the day. For the first believers, faith in Jesus did not cancel the need for these practices. He gave them their truest meaning.

Open the Book of Acts, and this reality is right there on the page. Luke doesn't even try to hide it. Centuries of Christian-centric bias have trained us to picture the first believers "leaving behind" their Jewish way of life, freed from the so-called burden of the law. But Luke paints the opposite picture: the earliest disciples saw no conflict between worshipping the Messiah and keeping the Torah God had given to Israel.

Before we look at specific examples from Acts, we need to step back and see the world they lived in—where they gathered, who was in their congregations, and why Jewish worship remained the heartbeat of their daily life.

WHEN FAITH IN JESUS WAS JEWISH

It's critical to recognize that in the first years after his ascension, faith in Jesus was a *Jewish phenomenon*. The vast majority of those confessing Jesus as Messiah in the first century were *Jews*. Gentile believers certainly existed, but they were the minority—and often in the earliest years the anomaly.

Faith in Jesus has always been a Jewish movement. It still is.

Today, more Gentiles follow him than Jews, but that doesn't erase the movement's roots. To read the New Testament rightly, we must stay anchored to this reality.

There were no Christians in the first century. Peter and James were Jews. Paul didn't leave Judaism to 'join Christianity,' and he wasn't running around persecuting Christians. Imagining the early believers in Acts as Christians is historically misleading. It forces their story into modern categories that hadn't yet developed. Even the term itself didn't yet exist, at least in the way we use it today. "Christianoi" appears for the first time in Antioch (Acts 11:26), and not as a self-designation but a nickname outsiders used for a Jewish messianic group that had begun welcoming Gentiles.[18] At that stage, it was still understood as a sect within Judaism—not a new religion. Only later, as Gentile numbers grew and the movement spread through the Roman world, did "Christian" come to describe a distinctly Gentile community and faith practice.

This Jewish-style faith in Jesus was lived out in two places: the Jerusalem temple and the synagogues scattered across the Roman world. Like today, many Jews lived outside Jerusalem, and the synagogue was their hub of worship and community. There, Jews first heard the news about Jesus—and Gentiles encountered him through synagogues for the first time as well.

In fact, Gentiles were no strangers to Jewish gatherings. Many were drawn to the morals, monotheism, and rich traditions of Judaism, so it was not unusual to find them in synagogues. Picture a first-century synagogue on Sabbath. Jewish families arrive first; Gentiles slip in to the side. Drawn by Israel's God, they sit apart, listening as Torah is read and prayers rise. They weren't outsiders to synagogue life—they learned, worshipped, even joined in festivals. So when the news of Jesus spread through these networks, Gentiles heard it too. Many embraced him, and in some cities, Gentile numbers grew. But in the early years, the core remained Jewish.

Almost every city in the Roman world had at least one synagogue; many had several. Like modern Christian churches, synagogues were united by shared core beliefs but represented different streams or denominations within first-century Judaism.[19] Pharisees prized Torah study; Sadducees guarded the temple and denied certain beliefs like resurrection. The Essenes were a separatist group committed to rigorous purity and communal living. Others reflected Hellenistic Judaism— communities of Greek-speaking Jews shaped by life in the wider Roman world. Hellenists were not a separate sect in belief but more of a cultural group within Judaism, and you could find them mixing in all over. First-century Judaism was diverse—much like Christianity is today.

By Paul's day, some synagogues had even become known for their allegiance to Jesus.[20] Inside them, you'd find three groups side by side:

- Natural-born Jews: ethnic Jews, raised in Torah, circumcised on the eighth day. Paul himself was one (Phillippians 3:5).

- Converts: Gentiles who converted to Judaism through immersion, Torah observance, and circumcision, gaining legal and religious standing as Jews.

- God-fearers: Gentiles who stopped short of conversion but embraced synagogue life and became friends of the Jewish people. These Gentile God-fearers embraced Jewish Sabbath, festivals, prayer, and other customs. They were not obligated to keep the Torah, but many still participated in Jewish worship traditions. Some eventually converted, while others remained on the fringes, navigating the tension between Jewish worship and Roman civic religion.[21]

Paul himself greets all three groups in the synagogue at Pisidian Antioch: ***"Brothers, sons of Abraham's family,*** *and those among you who **fear God***" (Acts 13:26). In one sentence, he speaks to natural-born Jews: his "brothers," Jewish converts: sons of Abraham's family, and God-fearing Gentiles: "you who fear God."[22]

For years, I pictured the early believers gathered in something like a church basement, far removed from the temple or synagogue. My understanding of Acts was shaped by well-meaning sermons and study guides that imagined the first "converts" leaving Jewish spaces behind for new "Christian" gatherings. But Acts tells a different story: Jews who believed in Jesus stayed rooted in Jewish worship, and Gentiles entered through the same gate. Faith in Jesus grew inside Judaism, not outside it.

HOW THE FIRST BELIEVERS BECAME CHRISTIANS (IN OUR IMAGINATION)

Over time, something shifted in how that story was remembered. The Jewish movement that had welcomed Gentiles eventually came to be seen—and remembered—as a new religion that left Judaism behind. But the first believers didn't see themselves as Christians in the way we use that word today. It's worth pausing to ask how we came to imagine that they did.

After the temple's destruction in 70 CE, Jewish life—within and beyond the Jesus movement—had to adapt to persecution and the loss of a central place of worship. In the Roman world, communities with legal recognition fared better than those without. As Gentile-majority assemblies grew and synagogues faced increasing pressure, tensions deepened. Gentiles, for understandable reasons, began to distance themselves from the Jewish people. What had been an overtly Jewish sect that welcomed Gentiles slowly became, in the empire's eyes and eventually its own, a separate religion (and one that was not a threat to Rome). The Sabbath was moved to Sunday, biblical festivals gave way to Christian holidays, and Jewish worship was replaced by a new liturgy with new meanings—ones that evolved from Jewish tradition but transformed it into something recognizably different.

As Gentile-led gatherings developed their own ways of teaching, praying, and celebrating the faith—largely apart from the Torah-centric practice that had birthed them—those forms came to be seen as the superior and enlightened expression of faith in Jesus. Over time, creeds, catechisms, and the writings of influential leaders formalized these practices into a distinct identity. The story of Israel's Messiah was retold through the theology of the Gentile Church—shaped by Greco-Roman thought and increasingly filtered through supersessionism.

When studying church history, it doesn't take long to see that something went wrong very early on. Anti-Jewish sentiment spread during the second and third centuries, fueled by the Roman world's reaction to Jewish revolts and uprisings. The writings of some of the earliest church fathers reveal a troubling stance toward Jewish tradition and its people.[23] Despite Paul's clear teaching that Gentiles were being welcomed into the commonwealth of Israel (Ephesians 2:12), influential Gentile believers quickly began to tarnish any Jewish expression of faith in Jesus—a shift that tragically helped lay the groundwork for some of the worst antisemitism the world has ever seen. It's a dark reality within Christianity that many believers are unaware of.

Much has been written on this topic in recent decades, beyond the portrait we find in Acts. Still, both Jews and Christians have, for different reasons, largely rejected this middle-ground expression of faith that sought to honor the organic link between Judaism and belief in Jesus as Messiah. As a result, the story of the earliest believers—their lived faith and practice—has largely vanished from history and been recast within Christian imagination as polemic.[24] The portrait of the apostles and earliest believers most Christians know today has been shaped less by what the New Testament records and more by how later church fathers remembered and interpreted them.[25] In that retelling, the earliest believers came to look like Christians rather than Torah-faithful Jews. What began as a Jewish movement, rooted in Jewish practices and proclaiming Israel's Messiah, gradually came to be remembered as the origin story of a new religion founded by Jesus.

The very first believers, however, lived well before Christian tradition took shape. They lived and worshiped as Jews, or as Gentiles integrated to at least some degree within Jewish community. When we anachronistically cast them as Christians in the modern sense, we obscure the very lens that shaped their faith: the Torah, the temple, the synagogue, and the shared table. That loss matters, because it quietly removes a Levitical chord from their gospel—and from ours.

ACTS 2–THE LEVITICAL CALENDAR IN ACTION

With this background in view, it's not surprising to find the disciples of Jesus still gathering at the temple on Israel's holidays. They hadn't stepped away from Jewish life at all (at least not in the earliest years).[26] "When the day of Pentecost arrived, they were all together in one place …" (Acts 2:1) This is one of the most famous moments in the New Testament, yet some critical details are often overlooked.

"Pentecost" is simply the Greek name for Shavuot, the Feast of Weeks, the final spring festival in Israel's liturgical calendar (Leviticus 23:15–22). Shavuot wasn't an isolated holiday. It was the finale of the spring feasts that began with Passover, Unleavened Bread, and Firstfruits about fifty days earlier. From the offering of first barley sheaves at Firstfruits, Israel literally counted each day—seven full weeks—until the wheat harvest ripened. At Shavuot, priests offered two lambs along with fully baked, leavened loaves of wheat bread, waved before the Lord in thanksgiving for the harvest. It was a feast of God's provision and a celebration of the season's abundance, with the crop of figs, grapes, pomegranates, and olives soon to follow.

In the first century, these rituals unfolded in and around the temple complex in Jerusalem. Shavuot, like Passover and Tabernacles, was a pilgrimage festival. A representative from every Jewish family within the diaspora was expected to come to the temple to worship. Luke's audience, of course, knew this. When Luke tells us the disciples were "all together in one place," he doesn't need to specify where. It's implied. They were almost certainly at the temple, not hiding in the private upper room of Acts 1. The "house" the Spirit filled was the *house of the Lord*, the most common biblical way of referring to the temple itself.

I realize this may be a tough leap for some of us to make, but the tension lies in our own traditions of telling the story, not in Luke's account.

His description of Pentecost places the event squarely within Jewish worship, not outside it. These disciples hadn't abandoned Judaism or invented a new faith—this was only weeks after Jesus's crucifixion. They were still praying in the temple, observing the festivals, and living as faithful Jews.[27] To imagine them already forming a separate religion dismisses the picture Luke goes out of his way to show and lifts the biblical festival of Shavuot out of its first-century context.

Try to picture it: the temple courts are buzzing with travelers from across the Jewish world—Judea, Galilee, Asia Minor, Egypt, Rome—each speaking their own native language. Priests are leading prayers, preparing offerings, and waving bread before the altar. Then, without warning, the sound of a rushing wind fills the air, and tongues of fire appear over the heads of the disciples. The Spirit falls, not in a hidden corner, but right within the heart of temple worship on Shavuot.

On the day Israel celebrated God's provision and the first fruits of the wheat harvest, the Father gathered the first fruits of a far greater harvest—Jewish men and women from every corner of the diaspora, filled with his Spirit, ready to go bear fruit for his kingdom. Luke tells us that these were ". . . devout men from every nation under heaven" (Acts 2:5), Torah-faithful pilgrims who had traveled great distances to be in Jerusalem for Shavuot. When the disciples began speaking in other languages, each heard the wonders of God—and the testimony of Jesus—in their own native tongue. Three thousand Jews believed Peter's message that day, right in the midst of a commanded Levitical festival and the sacrificial worship of the Temple.

The symbolism is beautiful. Just as Shavuot marked the first fruits of the wheat harvest, the Spirit's outpouring marked the first fruits of Messiah's worldwide harvest—destined to start with the Jewish people and spread to the ends of the earth. And notice this: even after following Jesus for years, witnessing his resurrection, and seeing him ascend, his disciples were still worshipping at the temple, still keeping the feasts, still honoring the calendar God gave Israel in Leviticus. For them, the Messiah didn't replace these things. He brought them to their fullest meaning.

PETER AND JAMES: JEWISH LEADERS LIVING LEVITICAL LIVES

The Spirit's outpouring at Shavuot was not the start of a movement that abandoned Israel's ways. Nowhere is this fact more visible than in the lives of the movement's earliest leaders, Peter and James. From the beginning, they modeled how to follow Jesus while staying deeply rooted in Jewish worship. They never set aside the Torah's commands. They kept living as observant Jews—only now, their faith in the Messiah infused those practices with new depth and meaning.

Luke shows Peter and John still walking up to the temple for the afternoon prayers (Acts 3:1), tied to the daily sacrifices in Leviticus 6. This wasn't a casual stop. They were joining the same liturgy their ancestors had kept for centuries, praying at the very hour when offerings rose for Israel.

Peter's own letters reflect the same alignment with God's standards. He calls believers to "be holy in all your conduct" because "it is written, 'You shall be holy, for I am holy'" (1 Peter 1:15–16), quoting directly from Leviticus 19. He urges them to abstain from sinful desires, conduct themselves honorably among the nations, and live as a "royal priesthood" offering spiritual sacrifices to God (1 Peter 2:5, 9, 11–12)—language steeped in Levitical imagery.

Even Peter's famous vision in Acts 10, often misunderstood as permission to abandon the kosher food laws, fits this pattern. The text never says that Peter stopped keeping the Torah's dietary commands. In fact, when told to kill and eat, he protests, "I have never eaten anything common or unclean." The vision itself explains the meaning: God was commanding Peter not to consider Gentiles "unclean" or to hesitate in sharing fellowship with them. This became clear when Peter was invited to the home of Cornelius, a Roman centurion and Gentile. While Peter almost certainly shared a meal with Cornelius and his family—a practice he later wavered on, as Paul notes in Galatians 2—nothing suggests he abandoned a kosher diet. Such behavior would contradict his lifelong devotion to God and his leadership of the Jerusalem community.

James, the brother of Jesus and leader of the Jerusalem believers, is another example of Jewish devotion. James was a man of the temple. Historical accounts outside of the New Testament describe him as spending so much time in prayer there that his knees became calloused like those of a camel. In Acts 21:20–24, we see him urging Paul to join in purification rituals and sacrificial offerings—actions straight from the Levitical system—as a public demonstration of commitment to the Torah. This same belief shines throughout his letter. James exhorts believers to "fulfill the royal law according to the Scripture, 'You shall love your neighbor as yourself'" (James 2:8), quoting directly from Leviticus 19:18. He warns that failing in even one part of the Torah makes a person "guilty of all of it" (2:10), underscoring the Torah's ongoing authority and unity. (James was addressing primarily a Jewish audience here, but I'll address the question of Gentile observances of Torah in the next chapter.) Like his brother, James viewed the Torah as the standard for God's people and led the Jewish messianic community by example.

For Peter and James, following Jesus never meant leaving Leviticus behind. They prayed at the temple, kept the feasts, offered sacrifices, and lived by the Torah—leading a community that did the same.

PAUL'S LEVITICAL FAITH

If James was known for his devotion in the temple courts, Paul was no less committed to the life of a faithful Jew. Even after decades of ministry among the nations, Acts consistently portrays him taking vows, observing purification rites, and participating in temple rituals.

In Acts 21, Jerusalem believers worried about rumors from the diaspora—that Paul told Jews to forsake Torah. He hadn't. To silence the lies, James asked him to prove his Torah faithfulness: join purification rites and cover the expenses of four men completing vows. In short, they asked Paul to practice Leviticus. And he did, without hesitation.

In Acts 24:1–20, standing before a Roman governor, Paul made his Jewish identity unmistakable. He described himself as a worshipper of "the God of our fathers," believing "everything laid down by the [Torah] and written in the Prophets," holding fast to the Pharisaic hope of resurrection, and bringing alms and offerings to Jerusalem. He emphasized that he had been found in the temple "purified," without causing any disturbance, and that his life remained firmly rooted in authentic Jewish worship.

Like Peter's vision in Acts 10, Paul's words in 1 Corinthians 9 ("all things to all people") are often misunderstood as if he set aside Torah or only pretended to be Jewish when it suited him. But Paul was not a swindler who compromised his Jewish faith. Rather, he sought common ground without compromising his identity and convictions as a practicing Jew.

To Jews, he spoke and lived in ways that reflected his shared heritage. To Gentiles, he relaxed customs where he could to prevent unnecessary barriers, but never gave up the moral or Jewish-specific standards of Scripture. For example, before Jerusalem's educated leaders, he high-lighted his own Pharisaic training to earn their respect (Acts 22:1–2). When under Roman custody, he invoked his citizenship to avoid an unlawful flogging (Acts 22:25–29). Paul could function comfortably in both Jewish and Gentile settings, but his adaptability was never a departure from the Torah that defined his life.

Perhaps one of his most striking self-disclosures comes in 2 Corinthians 11:24: "Five times I received from the Jews the forty lashes minus one." It's easy to imagine this scene as a "converted" Paul being attacked by an angry mob for believing in Jesus—like a man whipped in a back alley. But the "forty lashes" was a specific penalty outlined in Deuteronomy 25:1–3, administered only after formal judgment in a Jewish court. The point of the punishment was restorative: to remove guilt, restore honor, and reinstate the guilty party to full standing in Jewish community. The law itself protected the offender from excessive degradation, explicitly reminding the judge that the offender was still "your brother."

For Paul to receive this punishment, he had to present himself before a Jewish court, be judged guilty according to Torah, and consent to the lashes. Paul did this five different times. This was not the treat-ment given to apostates or blasphemers, but to members of the Jewish community who wanted to remain within it. Paul's repeated willingness to undergo this punishment reveals how deeply he valued his standing as a Jew. If he had abandoned his Jewish identity after coming to faith in Messiah, there would have been no reason to endure such an ordeal.

Far from being a "bad Jew" who converted to Christianity, Paul's faith in Jesus remained Torah-centric to the end. His life was not just consistent with Leviticus—it was proudly marked by it. After years of hardship, missionary travel, and persecution, Paul could still stand before a Roman governor and affirm with confidence that his worship, hope, and obedience were rooted in the same Torah and Prophets that had shaped his own life and his people for centuries.

GENTILE GOD-FEARERS PRACTICING TORAH: AN ETHIOPIAN EUNUCH, CORNELIUS, AND LYDIA

Luke doesn't just record the Jewish faith-practice of the apostles. He also highlights Gentiles who worshipped Israel's God through the patterns and constructs of the Torah. These God-fearers were not independent "seekers" who stumbled into faith in Jesus. They were already rooted in the worship practices of the Jewish community: learning the Scriptures, prayers, and liturgies of Israel. Their encounters with the gospel came within that setting.

One such example appears in Acts 8: the Ethiopian eunuch. A high-ranking official in charge of the treasury of the queen of Ethiopia, he had traveled an enormous distance to bring gifts to Jerusalem. There, he had likely joined other God-fearers in prayer and study. On his return journey, he was still immersed in the Torah and Prophets—muddling his way through Isaiah's scroll—when Philip met him. This man's pilgrimage, generosity toward Israel, and devotion to Scripture show him as a Gentile already shaped by Jewish worship. When Philip explained how Isaiah pointed to the Messiah, the eunuch eagerly embraced Jesus within the very Jewish framework he had come to love.

Cornelius, who hosted Peter in Acts 10, was a Roman centurion in the Italian cohort—a man of rank and influence. Luke describes him as "devout" and a "God-fearer," someone who gave generously to support the Jewish people and prayed continually. His prayers were not random moments of personal meditation. They aligned with the formal Jewish hours of prayer. The "ninth hour," when Cornelius prayed and received his vision, was the time of the evening sacrifice in the Jerusalem temple. Even in the diaspora, Jews and God-fearers alike oriented their prayers toward Jerusalem at those times. Cornelius's habits were not innovations of his own. They were traditions he learned within the synagogue and Jewish community he belonged to.

Lydia appears in Acts 16, where Paul is traveling in Philippi. This city had no synagogue, but Paul sought out a place where Jews might gather for shabbat worship on a Saturday morning. He found it at the riverbank, a likely meeting spot for prayer when a formal synagogue was unavailable. There Paul met Lydia, a wealthy merchant from Thyatira. Though Gentile by birth, she was a worshipper of the God of Israel, joining other women in keeping shabbat. Her faith was already shaped by Torah-centric worship long before Paul arrived. When she heard the message of Jesus as Messiah, she responded immediately, receiving baptism—a cleansing ritual familiar to her from the Levitical teachings she already knew.

There is no reason to believe that any of these Gentiles ever abandoned the Jewish practices they had embraced as God-fearers. For them, belief in Jesus was not a freedom from Torah-shaped worship. They had learned to love Israel's God through Jewish example and the Hebrew Scriptures, and their faith in Messiah grew naturally out of that soil. Even without being obligated to keep the Torah, they gladly participated as they could, seeing it as a way to honor the God who had now revealed his Anointed One to them.

TORAH AT THE TABLE

Having recovered the identity and practice of the first believers, it's worth pausing to consider one more central form of worship drawn straight from Leviticus: their table fellowship. Wherever they lived, in

Jerusalem or beyond, the table remained the heartbeat of worship for the Jesus movement. This was no innovation born at Pentecost or instituted by Jesus at the Last Supper, but a deeply Jewish tradition rooted in Leviticus. In Leviticus 1–7, offerings are called holy or most holy based on who may eat them and where. Some were reserved for priests, others shared by the worshipper, and still others eaten in joy before the Lord. In Leviticus, eating itself is an act of worship.

That rhythm runs through all of Scripture—from Abram and Melchizedek's bread and wine (Genesis 14), to the Passover meal (Exodus 12), the fellowship offerings (Leviticus 6–7), the table imagery of the Psalms (Psalm 23), and the marriage supper of the Lamb (Revelation 19). From beginning to end, sharing a meal before God is how his people draw near to him.

Like all other Jews, the first believers lived this truth in their homes. They broke bread and gave thanks, (the very meaning of *eucharistein*, from which we get *Eucharist*) blessing God in the same pattern their ancestors had followed for centuries. The head of the household would take bread, pronounce the *berakhah or blessing* ("Blessed are You, Lord our God, King of the universe"), break it, and distribute it. The New Testament idiom "breaking bread" can refer to any meal, and *eucharisteo* simply means "to give thanks," describing the standard Jewish blessing during a meal.

In other words, the apostles weren't creating a new ritual to transcend temple sacrifice—they were continuing a deeply Jewish form of worship. New Testament references to communal "love feasts" (1 Corinthians 11; Jude 12) show that these meals could take different cultural forms—some likely following Jewish custom, others reflecting a more Greco-Roman banquet style—but all centered on shared fellowship and thanksgiving to God. Nothing in the New Testament suggests these gatherings were meant to replace Levitical or temple worship. The bread and wine reminded them of what Jesus had done, just as the matzah and wine at Passover recalled God's redemption of their ancestors.[28] Only later did the church give those gestures sacramental weight—lifting them from their Passover roots and interpreting them as the fulfillment or alternative to temple sacrifice.[29] The apostles themselves, in those earliest decades, likely held no such fully developed meaning; they were continuing Jewish worship around a shared meal, and later generations carried those practices forward into fuller sacramental expressions.

Over time, the church's table practice took on new forms and a different tone as it sought to distinguish itself from Judaism. The danger today isn't this diversity, but forgetfulness—imagining a Christian version of the Lord's Table where none originally existed. When we treat communion as a replacement for (or superior to) the table fellowship the New Testament records, it's easy to lose its original meaning and to read our later traditions back into their story. To share in the Lord's Table as a believer is a beautiful act of worship and faith, regardless of the tradition behind it. It is equally beautiful to recover the bread and cup as Jesus and the first believers shared it: a home table, a festive meal, a family blessing, and gratitude offered in the presence of God—with the added reminder of all Jesus has done to gather the multi-ethnic family of God as one.

FINAL THOUGHTS

Luke's portrait of the first believers is anything but generic. What we see in these pages is truly remarkable: for roughly the first fifty years, faith in Jesus was a thoroughly Jewish phenomenon. Gentiles were welcomed in, and temple and Levitical worship continued right alongside their confession of Jesus as Messiah. Judaism and Christianity would later pull apart for different reasons, but that early, organic link still has something to teach us—if we have the ears to hear it.

These men and women, whether born Jewish or drawn in as Gentile God-fearers, followed Jesus while living fully immersed in Torah culture. James prayed daily in the temple. Paul submitted to purification rites. Cornelius prayed at the hour of sacrifice. Peter preached the Messiah in the temple courts. Lydia joined a shabbat gathering by the river. The first believers shared meals together, remembering Jesus around the table at home. The picture is unmistakably Jewish: these early communities did not see the Messiah as the end of Levitical worship, but as the reason for it.

If Jesus's death truly ended the need for all things Leviticus, it must also have ended them for the first believers. But it didn't. They confessed Jesus as Messiah, just as we do today. They believed in his sinless life, atoning death, and life-giving resurrection—yet they still offered sacrifices and lived by Torah. From temple courts to sabbath tables, this was the world where faith in Jesus first lived—a world alive with Levitical rhythms.

Luke's portrait reminds us that the first believers never saw a contradiction between confessing Jesus as the Messiah and living Torah-centered lives. They practiced Leviticus because its story had always been the way to draw near to God. Somewhere along the way, we lost that vision. In our eagerness to escape what we thought were old statutes and ways, we cast a Christian shadow where there wasn't one. The earliest believers knew better. In their eyes, Jesus didn't cancel Leviticus. He illuminated its traditions with new meaning, filling their worship with the hope of a risen Messiah.

8

PAUL AND THE TORAH

PAUL IS SOMEWHAT OF A PUZZLE. On one page of the New Testament, he's in the temple making offerings, taking vows, and calling himself a Pharisee. On the next, he seems to thunder against the law: "You are not under law but under grace" (Romans 6:14), "Christ is the end of the law" (Romans 10:4), "the law was our guardian until Christ came" (Galatians 3:24).

Which is it? Was Paul the Torah-keeping Jew or the Torah-dismantling apostle? Both pictures can't be right. Generations of readers have wrestled with this tension, and most settled for a reading that makes Paul the founder of Christianity, not the faithful Jew that Acts portrays. But what if the real problem isn't Paul at all? What if the problem is our lens for understanding his letters?

Instead of pulling every proof text in the New Testament in which Paul seems to condemn the Torah, we'll let Acts, Paul's Jewish identity, and his world guide us in understanding him. That means recovering four things:

- The Author: Who was Paul, really?

- The Audience: Who was he writing to?

- The Issue: What challenges were these early communities facing?

- The Terminology: How did Paul speak to those challenges in their own categories?

Read this way, Paul's letters don't dismantle the Torah or Leviticus. They align perfectly with his own life, with the account of Acts, and with the authority Jesus gave the Torah.

RECOVERING THE AUTHOR

Paul never stopped being Jewish. I won't belabor the point of the previous chapter, except to say that if we have any hope of understanding Paul, we must stay connected to this reality. Like the first believers before him, Paul's faith in Jesus did not end his Jewish identity—it reoriented it around the conviction that Israel's Messiah had come.[30]

Tradition remembers him as the man who broke away from Judaism to start Christianity, but that picture doesn't match his own words or his life. What Paul embodied was not a rejection of Judaism, but one particular expression of it within the rich diversity of Second Temple life. Still, he was a Torah-observant Jew. Of course, he made concessions where possible—like eating at the same table as Gentiles—but that doesn't mean he went wild for pulled pork sandwiches. He didn't abandon his identity the way we might imagine an Amish person "leaving the old ways" for secular culture. His adaptations were missional, not theological—ways of building bridges without breaking covenant.

Decades after meeting Jesus, Paul still called himself "a Pharisee, a son of Pharisees" (Acts 23:6). He reminded the Romans that he was "an Israelite … from the tribe of Benjamin" (Romans 11:1). To the Philippians he bragged, "Circumcised on the eighth day … a Hebrew of Hebrews" (Philippians 3:5). Far from leaving his Jewish ways behind, Paul wore Judaism as a badge of honor. He was born into Torah observance, raised in a devout Jewish home, and trained to zealously defend the traditions of his fathers (Galatians 1:14). In that sense, Paul stood within Judaism's ongoing conversation about how best to live faithfully under God's covenant in a changing world. His conclusions were radical, but they were not utterly foreign to that world.

Even his peers recognized his depth of insight. Peter admitted that Paul's letters were "hard to understand" because of the wisdom packed into them (2 Peter 3:15–16). Paul had an unbelievably deep grasp of the Hebrew Scriptures and Jewish rabbinic tradition, even surpassing other Jewish teachers. This wasn't the voice of an outsider inventing a new religion. It was the voice of a rabbi steeped in the Torah, convinced that Israel's Messiah had come.

Contrary to the popular image of Paul as the man who founded Christianity, he was not running around the Mediterranean spreading a new religion. Paul was spreading Judaism—specifically, the announcement that Jesus was Israel's long-awaited Messiah. Far from discarding his heritage, he considered the Jewish faith to be of immense value to the entire world: "What is the value of being a Jew? … Much in every way!" (Romans 3:1–2). "To [the Jews] belong the adoption, the glory, the covenants, the giving of the law, the worship, and the promises. To them belong the patriarchs, and from their race, according to the flesh, is the Christ, who is God over all, blessed forever. Amen" (Romans 9:4–5).

Paul's mission, however, set him apart. Paul was an apostle to the

Gentiles (Romans 11:13). While Peter, James, and John focused their ministry within the Jewish world, Paul was sent far beyond Jerusalem to proclaim Israel's Messiah to the nations. His heart burned to help non-Jews understand how Jesus was the fulfillment of Israel's ancient promises. This was not "Christianity" in the later sense, but Judaism in action—a Jewish apostle bringing the light of Israel's Scriptures to the nations.

This calling required him to translate the hope of the Torah and Prophets into terms the Gentile world could grasp, interpreting that hope through the reality of Israel's Messiah while staying true to the Torah he loved. He walked a line between two worlds—seeing the gospel anew in light of Jesus yet remaining anchored in the practices and worship of his people. In doing so, Paul faced unique challenges and tensions the other apostles rarely encountered.

This unique assignment is key to understanding Paul's letters. He often wasn't writing to people raised in the Torah from birth. His audiences came from a swirl of cultures and worldviews, and his words met them right in the middle of their own questions and obstacles as non-Jews learning to follow Israel's Messiah.

RECOVERING THE AUDIENCE

Paul's letters weren't written into a vacuum. They were tailored to the messy, mixed communities he served. Some gatherings, like those in Corinth, were heavily Gentile. Most, however, were Jewish-led synagogues scattered throughout the diaspora, where Jews and Gentiles worshiped together under Roman rule. Recall that inside these communities, you'd usually find three groups—natural-born Jews, converts to Judaism, and Gentile God-fearers. Paul's ministry touched all three.

For centuries, these groups had coexisted. Some God-fearers eventually converted; others remained in-between, Gentiles living on the edges of Jewish community. But in the days of the apostles, something new was beginning to take shape: Gentiles weren't just drifting into synagogues. They were confessing Jesus as Messiah in growing numbers.

The normal balance was starting to shift. Suddenly, Jewish communities had to wrestle with a question they'd never faced before: what happens when a wave of Gentiles claim Israel's Messiah and seek fellowship within the synagogue?

THE MAIN ISSUE

Paul confronted some massive, unprecedented questions in the first century. By far the biggest issue revolved around this question: Should Gentile believers be required to undergo legal conversion into Judaism in order to be considered righteous before God and inherit eternal life?

For modern Christians, this seems like an obvious "no." Thanks largely to Paul, we take for granted that a person can worship Jesus without being Jewish. But in the first century, the Jesus movement remained overwhelmingly Jewish, with a small but growing number of Gentiles joining their ranks. Faith in Jesus was still expressed within Jewish spaces—synagogues, homes, and festival gatherings—where Jews and Gentiles learned to worship together.

Jews within these synagogues were naturally cautious around Gentile believers. In first-century collectivist societies like the Roman Empire, maintaining clear boundaries between groups protected identity, honor, and cohesion. Group identity was everything. It marked a person's rank and social standing clearly.[31]

Jews were already struggling to preserve their identity in a Hellenized world, where intermarriage and secular culture blurred lines. So requiring Gentiles to legally convert to Judaism was a normal step for God-fearers who wanted to worship God to the fullest extent. As legal Jews, they could be fully embraced within Jewish community. In the apostolic era, conversion to Judaism didn't require renouncing faith in Jesus; Gentiles could convert through a recognized messianic sect like the Way.[32] There were long established protocols and rituals, and no one questioned the practice—except Paul.

Imagine the synagogue in Pisidian Antioch on a Sabbath (see Acts 13). Jews fill the benches, converts sit proudly as full members of Israel, and God-fearing Gentiles lean in at the edges. Paul's voice rises over the crowd, proclaiming that Israel's Messiah has come—and the room erupts with joy. Luke says "the Jews and devout converts" followed Paul and Barnabas, urging them to continue in God's grace (Acts 13:43) and invited them back to keep preaching the next Saturday. For a moment, it seemed the whole community was united.

But a week later when Paul returned, everything changed. "Almost the whole city gathered to hear the word of the Lord," Luke writes, "but when the Jews saw the crowds, they were filled with jealousy" (Acts 13:44–45). Within days, welcome turned to outrage. Paul was contradicted, slandered, and eventually driven out.

How could a message invited one week provoke outrage the next? What exactly was Paul teaching that drew such crowds and stirred such jealousy? Replacement Theology often frames this story as though the Jews and devout converts were jealous of God-fearing Gentiles who became the "new favorites" of God—implying that the Jews had rejected God and his Messiah while Gentiles flocked to faith in Jesus. But this misses the reality. In Acts 13, many in the synagogue responded positively to Paul's message. Luke says that "many of the Jews and devout converts followed Paul and Barnabas, who urged them to continue in the grace of God." They weren't rejecting Paul's claim about Jesus; they were at least open to it. Yet when large numbers of Gentiles gathered to hear him the following Sabbath, that's when jealousy flared and opposition began to form. And it doesn't appear that the presence of additional Gentiles caused the uproar—God-fearers had long been welcomed guests. The real offense was far more radical.

Paul taught a very specific and revolutionary gospel message: Gentiles could belong to the covenant family through faith alone in the Messiah *without becoming Jewish.*[33] No circumcision, no ritual immersion, no transfer of legal identity into Israel. Just faith in the Messiah. For many natural-born Jews raised in the Torah, and for converts who had willingly taken on its commands, this was unthinkable. Remember, collectivist cultures like those in Galatia fiercely guarded the boundaries of "us" and "them" because they define a person's place and preserve the group's social honor. Allowing Gentiles to "join the group" without following the centuries-old path threatened that order.

Gentile God-fearers occupied a no-man's-land in the first century: they worshipped Yahweh but remained Roman and were still required to participate in civic worship under Roman law. Conversion erased that ambiguity, clearly marking someone as Jewish and exempting them from Rome's imperial cult.

Paul's gospel shattered this system, striking at the heart of their way of life. The backlash was fierce. He was driven out of town, and by the next city, rumors had spread so widely that he was nearly stoned to death for this very belief. Requiring Gentiles to become Jewish revealed an earth-shattering theological problem for Paul. He was extremely distressed over the practice. In Galatians, he condemns it sharply, calling it "a different gospel" and pronouncing anyone who teaches it "accursed" (twice!).

In Paul's day, converting to Judaism was not merely changing religious affiliation, as it might be thought of today. Conversion in the first century was as much a legal transfer of identity as a religious and cultural change. A proselyte assumed the national identity of the Jewish people—becoming, in effect, a citizen of Israel, fully assimilated into Jewish life and accountable to Jewish law. For Paul, this posed a threat to God's promise to Abraham: if all Gentiles had to become Jewish, the blessing intended for all *nations* would collapse.

Paul's conviction was radical. He believed that the Torah itself anticipated Gentile inclusion *as Gentiles* (Galatians 3:8). He saw the Messiah as the one who tore down the wall of hostility between Jews and Gentiles—not by erasing the Torah, but by making space for nations to join Israel's God without losing their distinct identity. This was the gospel he championed: Jew and Gentile together, one but not the same through faith in the Messiah.

ADDRESSING THE BIG ISSUE–A PAULINE GLOSSARY

To explain this to his audiences, Paul relied on a handful of key terms, repeated again and again. The trouble is, we often read them through a Christian lens, shaped by centuries of tradition—especially the Reformation's debates over "faith vs. works." That's understandable; I did the same thing for years.

I thought *works* meant "earning salvation through keeping the Old Testament law," contrasted with *faith* as "trusting Jesus's sacrifice alone." Those categories matter in Christian theology, but they are not the categories Paul himself was working with. Paul wasn't a Christian. He wasn't debating these things in the way we imagine. He was a Jew in the first century, using Jewish terms to answer questions in his day— questions very different from ours.

What we think Paul means is often very different from what I believe Paul actually meant. Over time, I've compiled a "Pauline Glossary" to track his usage of various repeated terms and recover a more authentic meaning.

Justified = Legally Exonerated Before God

I used to think "justified" was just another word for "forgiven" or "saved." It's more precise. Think of a courtroom. Assume you're guilty of a crime, but your lawyer pleads your case and the judge pronounces you "not guilty." You still did the act, but the law no longer holds it against you.

That's Paul's picture. We are guilty of sin, but when we give allegiance to the Messiah, God declares us *exonerated*. Justification is the verdict that frees us from death's penalty.

Circumcision = A Legally Jewish Person

In Paul's world, "circumcision" wasn't simply a surgery—it was shorthand for *legal Jewish identity*. By birth or by official conversion, circumcision marked someone as a Jew. So when Paul warns against "the circumcision party" (Galatians 2:14, elsewhere called the *Judaizers*), he means those pressuring Gentile believers to become legally Jewish in order to be counted righteous. That was the norm in first-century

Jewish life: God-fearing Gentiles often converted, with circumcision, ritual immersion, and Torah observance sealing their new legal status. Paul rejected that requirement—not Torah observance itself, but the claim that legal Jewish identity was the key to a person's *exoneration* before God.

Works of the Law = Jewish Identity Markers

Traditionally, this phrase is read as "obeying the Torah to earn salvation." That's not what Paul meant. In his context, "works of the law" referred to specific commands of the Torah that marked a person as legally Jewish—circumcision (for males), dietary boundaries (keeping kosher), Sabbath observance as a covenant sign for Israel, participation in temple obligations, and visible signs such as tassels (*tzitzit*), or among the more devout, *tefillin* and other distinct garments of covenant identity.[34] By "works of the law," Paul is not referring to faithful obedience to the Torah or to the ordinary practices of first-century faith in Jesus, which at that time still looked very Jewish. Paul is not concerned that Gentiles might pray at the hours of prayer, rest on shabbat,[35] or participate in a festival. Gentiles had always done those things. Paul never once condemns it. His concern was Gentiles being pressured to undergo *legal conversion* and take on identity markers as if those things guaranteed righteousness.[36]

So when Paul insists "no one is justified by works of the law," he's not condemning Torah traditions in general. He's rejecting the idea that Jewish identity markers—by themselves—could exonerate anyone before God.[37]

RE-READING PAUL WITH HIS GLOSSARY

Armed with these definitions, many of Paul's familiar lines take on fresh clarity. Below, I've included the verses as written, but inserted the meaning in [brackets] alongside to keep his intent front and center.

- Galatians 2:15–16: "We are Jews by birth, not Gentile sinners; yet we know that [whether legally Jewish or not] a person is not justified [exonerated] by works of the law [the aspects of the Torah that confer legal Jewish identity] but through Christ Jesus [the Messiah's faithfulness]."

Paul asserts that even Jews by birth are exonerated by the Messiah, not by their Jewishness.

- Romans 3:28–4:6: "One is justified [exonerated before God] by faith, apart from the law [the aspects of the Torah conferring Jewish identity]. Is God only the God of Jews? Not at all—he is also God of Gentiles, who are justified [also exonerated] through faith. Do we overthrow the law [the Torah] by this faith? By no means! On the contrary, we uphold the law [the Torah]. Abraham's faith was counted as righteousness, apart from the law [the things marking him as Jewish]."

Faith doesn't nullify the Torah—it establishes it.

- Galatians 5:2–4: "I, Paul, say to you that if you accept circumcision [become legally Jewish], Christ [Messiah] will be of no advantage to you. I testify again to every man who accepts circumcision [undergoes legal conversion] that he is obligated to keep the whole law. You are severed from Christ [Messiah], you who would be justified [exonerated] by the law [the commands of the Torah that confer Jewish identity]; you have fallen away from grace.

Here, Paul warns that legal conversion was not the path to covenant life.

- Ephesians 2:8–10: "By grace you have been saved through faith … not as a result of works [Jewish identity markers]."

Salvation is God's gift. The Torah still defines the "good works" prepared for us. Paul takes his claims about the Torah's purpose even further in Romans 10:4: "For Christ is the end of the law for righteousness for all who believe." The Greek word *telos* (end) can mean "goal," "aim," or "result," so we could just as accurately read this verse as: "Messiah is the goal of the Torah, for righteousness for all who believe." In Galatians 3:23–25, Paul even compares the Torah to a *paidagōgos*, a caretaker: "Now before faith came, we were held captive under the law, imprisoned until the coming faith would be revealed. So then, the law was our guardian until Christ came, in order that we might be justified by faith. But now that faith has come, we are no longer under a guardian."

At first glance, this passage might make the Torah seem like a prison from which we've been freed. But Paul is not framing the Torah against faith. The *paidagōgos* he mentions was a guardian, often a trusted household servant charged with escorting the master's heir to and from their tutor, answering for their safety, and shaping their social conduct.

Paul's point is not that the Torah is a prison, but that it guarded and preserved God's people until faith in the Messiah came. Even the words "held captive" (*froureō*) and "imprisoned" (*sunkleiō*) convey protection and enclosure, like a shepherd's dog keeping the flock close until the shepherd arrives. For Paul, Torah and faith work together, leading God's people to the goal it always pointed toward: Messiah himself.

THE CONSISTENT PICTURE

When we step into Paul's world, his message is remarkably consistent:

- He never condemned Torah observance or Jewish worship.

- He never taught that Leviticus was obsolete.

- He never replaced the Torah or obedience to it with faith in Jesus.

Instead, he fought a specific battle: Gentiles belong in God's family by faith in Messiah, not by becoming Jews. Philippians 3 makes this explicit. Paul rehearses his credentials as a blameless Jew—circumcised, Hebrew of Hebrews, Pharisee—and then says: *But these markers alone don't resurrect you. Only Messiah does.*

The surprise was not that Gentiles could inherit eternal life. The surprise was that they could do this *as Gentiles.* They could retain their ethnic and legal identities, without going through the usual process of converting to Judaism. When we read Paul carefully, letting his own terms and context guide us, it becomes clear that his letters are not attacks on the Torah, but a radical defense of the Torah's own gospel—to welcome the Gentiles as Gentiles within Israel's promises.

THE COUNCIL OF JERUSALEM: JEW AND GENTILE LIVING OUT LEVITICUS TOGETHER

Paul pioneered the arguments that led to the Council of Jerusalem (Acts 15). His conviction that Gentiles did not need to convert came at great personal cost—he was persecuted and stoned for preaching this message. Even leaders like James and Peter were initially hesitant, but ultimately agreed (Galatians 2:2). At the Jerusalem Council, the apostles officially backed Paul. They insisted that righteousness comes through faith in the Messiah alone, while they themselves remained Torah-observant Jews.

The Jerusalem Council is often misread (especially among Evangelicals) as releasing Gentiles from Torah and Levitical law entirely. Most Protestant commentaries frame the Judaizers' message as "faith in Jesus *plus* works," and then claim that the apostles rejected works as part of salvation. That misses the point. The apostles absolutely believed that faith in Messiah must be lived in obedience—faith without works was no faith at all. What they opposed was forcing Gentiles to convert and assimilate into full Jewish identity. The real issue wasn't "faith versus works," but more "faith versus assimilation." The apostles' gospel required Gentiles to remain Gentile, living out their faith through the Torah's long-standing standards for non-Jews who had always worshipped alongside Israel.

The apostles said, "It has seemed good to the Holy Spirit and to us to lay on you no greater burden than these requirements: abstain from what has been sacrificed to idols, from blood, from what has been strangled, and from sexual immorality … If you keep yourselves from these, you will do well" (Acts 15:28–29). To modern believers, these may appear as warnings against pagan worship practices (and they were, even in their most ancient context). But first-century followers would have also recognized them as deeply Levitical, defining how to live in proximity to God.

Leviticus extends many rules and principles to "sojourners among you," that is, Gentiles living among ancient Israel. The apostles drew from Leviticus's guidance, applying its principles to the God-fearing Gentiles within the Jewish communities of their day. The dietary rules they imposed echo commands found all over Leviticus: life in the blood, proper draining (Leviticus 17), blood never to be consumed (3:17, 7:26–27), and avoidance of animals that die naturally or are torn by beasts (11:39–40). Sexual ethics reflect Leviticus 18, prohibiting incest, adultery, and other defiling acts. By applying these instructions to Gentiles, the apostles used Levitical wisdom to create a bridge for fellowship between Jews and Gentiles, showing that God's Torah extends beyond Israel and continues to shape righteous living for all who worship him.

The Jerusalem Council recognized that both Jews and Gentiles belong to God's family and that Torah standards had not been abolished for either group. Jewish believers were never told to abandon their worship or ways of life, and Gentiles were never asked to become Jews. Instead, the apostles instructed Gentiles to follow the Torah commands that had always applied to "sojourners," attaching themselves to the Torah culture of their day in appropriate ways, without becoming Jewish themselves. The council made it clear that no one was to judge Gentiles for what they ate or for the festivals they celebrated, but neither were Gentiles discouraged from participating in these things. They were welcomed into a Jewish faith in Jesus—sharing its worship and vision of faithfulness—without taking on the covenantal obligations of Jewish identity in order to be made right before God.

In Acts, the apostles issued these instructions broadly, without spelling out every detail of what counted as immorality or what qualified as "food strangled." Those definitions were already understood and distinctly Jewish in character. The apostles weren't creating a new Christian code of conduct, as Evangelicals often imagine. They were applying the Torah's vision of holiness to a diverse, multiethnic community that touched every aspect of life. (For a fuller discussion, see Appendix, part V.) These expectations were not about earning salvation but about Gentiles living faithfully within the covenant family of God.

The goal was unity. By observing these boundaries, Gentiles would avoid offending their Jewish brothers and sisters. The apostles weren't randomly picking a few Torah commands for Gentiles while discarding the rest. Rather, they drew wisdom from the story of Leviticus, using it to guide them as they worked to bring Jew and Gentile together in the unique challenges of their day.

Paul emphasizes the same principle, urging his communities to fulfill the "law of Messiah" by bearing with one another in their Torah practice. The "law of Christ" in Galatians is not Paul's replacement for Torah—it's mutual responsibility and grace within the messianic community. Naturally, tensions arose: Jews might see themselves as more devout, Gentiles might flaunt freedom in Messiah. Paul calls for honesty, humility, and compassion, guiding both groups to live faithfully according to Torah as it applied to them while supporting one another in this effort. "Let us therefore make every effort to do what leads to peace and to mutual edification" (Romans 14:10).

ONE FAMILY IN MESSIAH, BUT NOT THE SAME

Paul was so insistent about ethnic distinctions that he made it a rule. He wrote, essentially, "if you came to Messiah as a Jew, stay Jewish; if you came as a Gentile, stay Gentile. Your ethnicity doesn't determine your standing before God—faith does. But each person should live out that faith in the role God assigned" (paraphrase of 1 Corinthians 7:17–20).

Paul taught *Gentile inclusion* and *ethnic retention*. Believers were one family in the Messiah, but this oneness did not make them the same. In the Messiah, Jews and Gentiles were equal in regards to eternal life, standing, and value before God. Yet each carried distinct responsibilities and roles. Torah remained God's standard of righteous living—each group living according to the commands given to them by the Torah itself. Like a husband and wife unite as one flesh in marriage, but still retain their individual identities, both groups are one in the Messiah while maintaining the diversity and distinctions God created.

In much of Christian teaching, the phrase "there is no Jew or Greek" has been misunderstood to mean that Jewish believers cease being Jewish. They accept Jesus and become Christians. This teaches that, since all are the same in Messiah, Jewish expressions of covenant identity—such as circumcision, dietary laws, sabbath, or festival observances—are optional or irrelevant, effectively erasing Jewish identity. It says, *There is no distinction.* One Law theology (often recognized in the Hebraic Roots and some messianic traditions) goes in the opposite direction, asserting that Gentiles must adopt the full Torah, blending both groups into a homogenized identity. It implies, *We're all Israel now.*

Paul rejected both. His gospel declared Jew and Gentile are one in Messiah, but not the same.[38] Gentiles are welcomed into Israel's blessings in Messiah; Gentile vocation is allegiance to Israel's king and alignment with his ways, not ethnic Israel's covenant stipulations. That claim was the scandal. Paul wasn't persecuted simply for believing in Jesus, but for insisting that Gentiles could inherit eternal life without becoming Jewish, and that Jews should still remain Jews. One family, two identities—that was the radical gospel Paul preached, and it deeply offended many.

FINAL THOUGHTS–PIECING IT ALL TOGETHER

What I've just summarized in this chapter took years for me to uncover. I remain humbled by what I've learned. In all the sermons, Bible studies, and Protestant commentaries I encountered, no one ever showed me this side of Paul—his faithfulness to Torah, his Jewish identity, his mission to include the nations without erasing identities. The details are all in Acts, Paul's letters confirm them, historical records and scholarship verify the context—but Evangelical teaching rarely connected the dots. The apostles were not entering into our traditional faith vs. works debate. This is an important, but modern question shaped by the lens of Replacement Theology and the events of the Protestant Reformation.

The first-century question was much different: *did Gentile believers need to become legally Jewish to be made righteous before God and inherit eternal life in the world to come?* Paul and the other apostles said no. They were adamant that righteousness comes through faith in the Messiah alone, even though they were Torah-observant all their lives. For them, obedience to God meant living according to the Torah, which they upheld as God's standard for all believers.

Paul believed that Jesus's work on the cross destroyed the dividing hostility between Jew and Gentile, but did not destroy the Torah itself (Ephesians 2:14–15). The tensions of ethnicity, culture, and religious practice no longer needed to fracture and divide a Messiah-following community, but the distinctions themselves needed to remain. The apostles demonstrated that one family can honor God faithfully and live under the wisdom of the Torah while respecting the positions God assigned to each group.

The challenge for followers of Jesus today is that nearly two thousand years of history have eroded this vision. Many Evangelicals assume that Torah obedience is optional or irrelevant, forgetting that the apostles expected all believers—Jew and Gentile alike—to walk in the standards God outlined for them, respectively, in the Torah. Sadly, this has often left Jewish believers caught between two worlds—pressured to assimilate into Christian norms rather than embraced as a vital and unique part of Messiah's body. Tragically, we have neglected the apostles' call to honor both Jewish and Gentile identities in Messiah, to bear with one another, and to uphold Torah as a life-giving guide for faith.

Our Jewish brother Paul risked everything for us to remain non-Jewish while pledging allegiance to the Jewish Messiah. Imagine how our faith and love for Jesus might deepen if we embraced the apostles' understanding of Leviticus and the Torah in our lives. Would celebrating Passover make Jesus's death and resurrection even more meaningful to us? Would Tabernacles bring more joy than Christmas? Would it reshape how we pray? How and who we baptize? What moral and ethical standards would we hold differently? What aspects of knowing our Savior have we completely missed because of our blindness? While I do not have all the answers, I do believe these questions deserve careful, humble reflection.

At the very least, we owe our Jewish spiritual fathers the humility to read their letters sympathetically, to understand their audiences and contexts, and to evaluate our theology in light of their teachings. Where our beliefs diverge from their intent, we must allow the Holy Spirit to guide us in change and repentance, so that our faith aligns with the vision of unity and distinctiveness that our Messiah made possible.

9

WHAT ABOUT HEBREWS?

THE LETTER TO THE HEBREWS might be the hardest book in the New Testament to reconcile with Leviticus. On the surface, it seems to dismantle everything we've been tracing: the temple, Jewish expressions of worship, the sacrifices. For many, Hebrews is the final nail in Leviticus's coffin.

Traditionally, the letter is read as presenting Jesus as far superior to the earthly temple, to Moses and the Torah, and to the Levite priests, whose ministry and authority are now seen as unnecessary. He is also depicted as greater than the animal sacrifices, his once-for-all offering replacing them entirely. From this perspective, Hebrews seems to declare that Jesus made the Torah—and particularly the temple and its sacrifices—obsolete.

So we're left with a puzzle. Why would the letter dismiss the very system that Jesus, the apostles, and the earliest believers faithfully practiced? Why would an author who clearly knew the temple system so well suddenly disqualify it? Is Hebrews really the lone voice in Scripture that dethrones Leviticus?

But what if, once again, the problem isn't with Hebrews at all—but with the lens we've been using to read it? What if this letter, far from rejecting Leviticus, is the very key that ties it all together? Let's test that possibility. We'll start with what we know about Hebrews, then consider the historical context, the crisis it addresses, and see how its argument unfolds.

WHAT DO WE KNOW ABOUT HEBREWS?

The author and audience of Hebrews remain a mystery, but the letter itself gives us plenty of clues. A few points are almost universally agreed upon:

- The date: Written in the early 60s CE, while the temple still stood and Levitical worship was active.

- A sharp, apostolic author: The writer was closely tied to the apostolic community—if not an apostle himself. His voice carries authority, and his command of temple rituals shows firsthand familiarity. The mention of Timothy (Hebrews 13:22) places him squarely within the apostles' inner circle.

- A biblically literate Jewish audience: The letter assumes readers steeped in the Scriptures and fluent in rabbinic-style argument. Gentiles are scarcely mentioned, suggesting that the audience was primarily Greek-speaking Jews.

- Persecution and apostasy: Again and again, the author urges: *hold fast, don't drift, don't fall away.* This was a community staring down real pressure to abandon their confession of Jesus.

So far, it's straightforward. But when we press into the details, the picture gets contested.

- Where were the Hebrews located? Many scholars argue for Rome, citing Hebrews 13:24 and the persecution flaring from the area during this time. Others suggest the diaspora more broadly. An older tradition places them closer to home—in Judea, perhaps even Jerusalem itself.[39]

- Why were they persecuted? Christian tradition almost universally teaches that Hebrews was written to encourage "Jewish Christians" to remain steadfast in their faith despite persecution and pressures to revert to Judaism. Scholars typically suggest two possibilities: (1) the Hebrews were caving into pressure to return to Jewish practices as a means of earning salvation and avoiding persecution for believing in salvation through Jesus, or (2) they returned to Judaism to as a means of distancing themselves from persecution against Christians (the more prevailing view).

These are the standard views. But when you read Hebrews in its New Testament context, the popular interpretations start to fall apart. Many assume the letter teaches that the Levitical system is obsolete, but its pastoral heart and historical moment seem to tell a different story.

PROBLEMS WITH THE POPULAR READING

First, location. Hebrews is obsessed with the temple and its rituals. Most diaspora Jews lived far from Jerusalem; temple life wasn't their daily reality. But the letter's focus suggests that its audience likely lived in or near the city, where proximity allowed these Jews to engage in practices that were impossible for diaspora Jews. Hebrews 13:9–10 illustrates this: "It is good for the heart to be strengthened by grace, not by foods, which have not benefited those devoted to them. We have an altar from which those who serve the tent have no right to eat." This passage refers to sacrificial meat and bread that could only be obtained from the temple and had to be consumed in Jerusalem. Jews in the diaspora would have had little to no practical experience with this ritual. This suggests that the audience wasn't scattered abroad. They were more likely temple-going Jews, immersed in its rhythms week after week.[40]

Second, faith practice. The early Jesus-followers in Jerusalem never abandoned their Jewish way of life. Acts makes that crystal clear. So how could they be accused of "falling back" into something they had never left? And furthermore, no Jew of the first century believed that temple rituals were a ticket to salvation. Judaism does not teach this, nor does the Bible. Sacrifices purified space, kept God's dwelling clean, and restored worshippers to fellowship. They were never about earning eternal life.

Third, persecution. In the early 60s, there was no separate religion called Christianity to fall out of. Jesus's followers were still seen as a sect within Judaism—Jews and Gentile God-fearers who believed Israel's Messiah had come. The real targets of persecution were those who held this belief. What we now call "Christianity" was still recognized as a Jewish movement, not a rival to it. To say the recipients of Hebrews were "returning to Judaism" is anachronistic; it assumes that they had left Judaism in the first place. The biblical and historical evidence for this simply doesn't support that claim. What's more, leaning into Jewish practice would not have shielded them from danger. Roman hostility towards Jews was especially high during this period, and a so-called return to Judaism would have made them even more conspicuous.

A BETTER FIT

The popular interpretations don't fit the broader New Testament context. Yet Hebrews is still almost always taught as if its audience was "falling back into Judaism" to escape persecution. From there, the letter is framed as though its central aim was to discredit the temple, the priesthood, and the sacrifices—offering proof that Jesus is superior to them all and has rendered them obsolete.

But that's not what was happening. The early believers *were* under intense persecution for confessing Jesus as Messiah, and Hebrews speaks directly into that struggle. The crucial question is: who was persecuting them, and why?

Upon a careful examination, the evidence points not to a distant Roman crackdown but to Jewish believers in Jerusalem facing hostility from the very temple authorities who controlled their access to worship.

That context changes everything. Hebrews is not a warning against "sliding back into Judaism." It is a plea not to deny the Messiah, most likely to people under crushing pressure from the establishment that presided over the temple itself.

THE WORLD OF THE JERUSALEM BELIEVERS

Life for the early followers of Jesus in Jerusalem was never easy. Acts describes their joy and generosity, but also their poverty, famine, and constant pressure. And over them loomed an even greater threat: the Sadducees.

The Sadducees, rulers of the Sanhedrin and controllers of the temple, held the highest priestly seats and wielded enormous political power. They rejected resurrection, denied the Prophets, and clung to Torah alone. That put them in direct conflict with the apostles, who preached Jesus's resurrection as the climax of the entire Hebrew story. They regarded the apostles' proclamation of Jesus and his resurrection as a threat to their power.

Acts pulls no punches: "As they were speaking to the people, the priests and the captain of the temple and the Sadducees came upon them, greatly annoyed because they were teaching the people and proclaiming in Jesus the resurrection from the dead" (Acts 4:1). The Sadducees were not only jealous of the apostles' growing influence. They feared Rome. A messianic movement could spark rebellion and jeopardize their fragile alliance with imperial power. So they cracked down hard: arresting apostles, throwing believers into prison, seizing property, beating them, and orchestrating Stephen's violent stoning (Acts 5, 8).

Hebrews itself recalls this wave of early suffering: "After you were enlightened, you endured a hard struggle with sufferings … you joyfully accepted the plundering of your property, since you knew that you yourselves had a better possession and an abiding one" (Hebrews 10:32–34).

Then came the unthinkable. The believers' shared Jewish faith and confession of Jesus as Messiah challenged the authority of both temple leaders and political collaborators—even though they sought to live peaceably. A storm of violence was rising within Israel itself. Around 62 CE, James—the brother of Jesus and leader of the Jerusalem believers—was hurled from the pinnacle of the temple. When he miraculously survived the fall, they stoned him, and finally struck him dead with a club to the head.[41] His murder sent shockwaves through the community.

With James gone, the temple authorities had far greater leverage over the Jerusalem believers, who would have been deeply shaken by his loss. What better way to silence the rest than by threatening them with the ultimate penalty—banishment from the temple, or worse?

These early Jerusalem believers faced the very real threat of being barred from the temple—or worse fates—because of their conviction that Jesus was Israel's Messiah, a belief that directly challenged the Sadducees' authority. If they wanted to continue gathering as they always had, they faced enormous pressure to recant.

Losing access to the temple would have been devastating for a community already reeling from the humiliating loss of their leader. Where would they worship? How could they celebrate the festivals, offer sacrifices, or pray? They saw themselves as Jews. Their faith in Jesus had not erased their covenantal commitment to keep the Torah (Galatians 5:3), and without the temple, they felt they'd be cut off from representation before God through the priesthood.[42] What were they to do? Thus, they faced a pressing question:

Should they deny Jesus as Messiah to maintain their place in the temple, escape persecution, and keep their standing before God through the priesthood? It is likely into this crisis that the author of Hebrews speaks, urging them again and again:

- "Hold fast your confidence."

- "Do not harden your hearts."

- "We must pay closer attention … lest we drift away."

- "Do not neglect assembling together."

- "We have a sure and steadfast anchor."

Fear and uncertainty had brought them to the brink. Hebrews was written to pull them back.

THE POINT OF HEBREWS

Hebrews is not warning believers against slipping back into Judaism—they had never left it. The danger was far more costly. The author was concerned his audience would deny the Messiah and thereby forfeit their access to the *eternal* temple and *the world to come*.

At first, this can be easy to miss. Just trying to figure out the context of the letter is hard enough. But then, when we start reading the opening chapters of Hebrews, it can feel like being hit with a firehose—Messiah, angels, Moses, and constant Old Testament quotations all come at you in rapid succession. Modern readers can easily feel lost right in the few first paragraphs. We often respond by assuming the author's goal is simply to show that Jesus is better than all these old, Jewish things. That instinct is understandable, and it isn't entirely wrong. Hebrews does proclaim Jesus as the very revelation of God. But the author's point is not that Jesus replaces Israel's faith or worship—and the original audience would not have understood it that way.

What sounds to us like a complex argument against the temple or Leviticus would have landed entirely different to them. They were biblically literate Jews who recognized and understood every reference. It was not a critique, but a confirmation of their enduring purpose in light of the Messiah. For them, the author's opening words struck at this core issue. He hints at this issue early in chapter 2, but only briefly, almost in passing. The original audience didn't need it spelled out. We, however, do.

In the mind of the author, what is truly at stake for his audience is not access to the earthly temple, but access to "the world to come"—the eternal temple where Messiah reigns at God's right hand. "It is not to angels that he has subjected the world to come, about which we are speaking" (Hebrews 2:5, NIV). Did you catch that? *About which we are speaking.* From the very first lines, Hebrews is fixated on the world to come—and on who commands it. It's not the angels, temple authorities, Moses, or the prophets who hold its keys. It's the Messiah, the one at God's right hand.

To the Hebrews, the author says, *"Come on. You guys know the Psalms, the prophets. You know who's at the helm of the world to come, and **that's what we're really talking about here.**"* If the Hebrews denied Messiah now—yielding to temple authorities who threatened to expel them or worse—they risked forfeiting their inheritance in the world to come.

The modern Evangelical movement has shifted attention away from the world to come—the tangible renewal of creation, the restoration of Israel, and the reign of Messiah on earth—realities that stood at the very center of first-century faith. This concept can feel like a big leap for many of us. But for the audience, this hope was vivid and near: Messiah's reign, the resurrection, the greater temple, the ingathering of the scattered, the restoration of Jerusalem. These weren't abstract ideas; they were the very core of their worldview and their confession about Jesus.[43]

They didn't imagine his work ending at the resurrection. They anticipated his return through that eastern gate, ushering in the age and the world they longed to inherit. And here is the warning: if they denied Messiah to preserve their place in the earthly temple, they risked losing their share in the eternal one—the reality to which the earthly temple continued to point towards. The promised eternal temple didn't erase the earthly temple's function. Instead, the author used it as a living illustration to remind these shaken believers that God's presence would one day dwell fully with his people again.

That's why Hebrews pleads with such urgency: *Hold fast. Don't drift. Don't trade eternity for temporary relief.* To anchor them, the author turns again and again to Israel's own Scriptures. By revealing the depth of the Levitical system, he shows them that Jesus the key to everything they hoped for. And he explains it with a logic they could not miss.

THE LOGIC OF HEBREWS: A TALE OF TWO PUPPIES

Most Bible studies and teachings on Hebrews focus on how Jesus is better than the temple, better than the Levite priests, better than the sacrifices. Jesus is indeed of immeasurable value, but describing Jesus as *better* can carry unhelpful implications. Jesus is not better in the sense that all those things are obsolete and useless. He is better in the sense that *he is different.* He is greater because the office he holds is not merely for the things of this world, but for a *different, greater world to come.* Hebrews builds on this by using a simple logic pattern: the lesser thing magnifies the greater.

It works like this: if you give a child a stuffed puppy for their birthday and it becomes their favorite toy, imagine how much more excited would they be if you gave them a real puppy for Christmas. The joy of the lesser gift makes the joy of the greater believable. For the real dog to be of any value, the stuffed toy must first, of course, be of value. Hebrews uses this strategy everywhere:

- Torah compared with Jesus: If the words of the Torah, delivered through angels, hold such authority, how much more should we heed the Messiah, who speaks today? (Hebrews 1:1–2, 2:1–3)

- Moses compared with Jesus: If Moses was honored as a faithful servant in God's earthly house, how much more should we honor Jesus, the Son over God's eternal house? (Hebrews 3:1–6)

- Entering rest: If rebelling against Moses caused the wilderness generation to die outside the promised land, how much more serious is it to rebel against the Messiah, who holds the keys to God's eternal rest? (Hebrews 4:1–3,9–10)

- Earthly tabernacle vs. heavenly: If earthly rituals temporarily purified God's space on earth, how much more powerful is Messiah's blood for eternal purification in the world to come? (Hebrews 7:23–28)

- Animal sacrifices vs. Messiah's sacrifice: If animal sacrifices allowed temporary purity in the earthly temple, how much greater and more sufficient is Jesus's sacrifice for eternal access to God? (Hebrews 9:1–14)

Tradition often misreads Hebrews. If the letter dismissed the Levitical system, then by that logic, Jesus would also be obsolete—clearly not the case. Think of it like Christmas morning: a real puppy doesn't make the stuffed animal any less beloved. Try telling a child their favorite stuffed dog no longer matters now that they have a real one. You'll meet resistance. Each gift has its purpose; both have their place. They were never meant to compete.

This is exactly what Hebrews teaches. The earthly temple and its sacrifices were never failures; they were God's gifts, given for a specific purpose tied to the land and the temple the Hebrews cherished. Yet the author reassures them: even if they lose access to the earthly temple, they need not fear. Messiah himself is fulfilling these greater realities in a different temple, through a different priesthood, and with a different sacrifice in the heavenly realm—a realm destined to come to earth, "about which we are speaking" (Hebrews 2:5).

The heart of the matter is clear: if they want to have a part in that realm and world, they must hold fast to the Messiah here and now. Let's look at a few examples.

THE EARTHLY AND HEAVENLY TEMPLE: DIFFERENT TEMPLES FOR DIFFERENT REALMS

Hebrews draws on the Old Testament concept that there are two temples: one for earth and this age, and one for heaven and the age to come.[44] Two different temples for two different realms and ages.

Israel's earthly sanctuary was patterned after a heavenly one. When God instructed Moses to build the tabernacle, he stressed that it must match the heavenly "pattern" (Exodus 25:40, Numbers 8:4). The prophets confirm this: Isaiah saw the Lord enthroned in glory (Isaiah 6:1–3); Daniel beheld the Ancient of Days on his heavenly throne (Daniel 7:9–10). The Psalms echo the same truth: "The LORD is in his holy temple; the LORD's throne is in heaven" (Psalm 11:4). From the beginning, the earthly sanctuary was designed to mirror the one above.

Hebrews makes this point explicit: Levite priests "serve a copy and shadow of the heavenly things" (Hebrews 8:5), while the Messiah serves "in heaven itself" (Hebrews 9:24). In other words, the Jerusalem temple was a replica of the real, heavenly one. It serves a purpose for worship on the land, but it is not the temple where God will dwell forever. For the audience, this reminder was life-giving news. Even if they lost access to Jerusalem's temple, they had an advocate in the true temple—the Messiah himself. And that temple was not destined to remain in heaven forever. The prophets had already promised it would one day descend to earth, filling the New Jerusalem with God's presence in the age to come (Isaiah 60, Revelation 21:3).

From Eden to Sinai and onward, God's purpose is to dwell with his people (Exodus 29:45–46). The Hebrews needed to remember that this purpose would be fulfilled through the Messiah. Their hope was secure because of his ongoing service in the tent above, in the eternal city of God. "You have come to Mount Zion and to the city of the living God, the heavenly Jerusalem, and to innumerable angels in festal gathering, and to the assembly of the firstborn who are enrolled in heaven" (Hebrews 12:22–23).

THE DIFFERENT PRIESTHOOD FOR A DIFFERENT TEMPLE

If the temple is different, then the priesthood must be different as well. The Levites were chosen to guard and serve in the earthly sanctuary, but Jesus wasn't a Levite. Coming from the tribe of Judah, he was not qualified to serve in the earthly temple (and he never tried to). Instead, Hebrews identifies him with another priestly order altogether: Melchizedek's priesthood.

Melchizedek appears suddenly in Genesis 14 as both priest and king, blessing Abraham and receiving tithes from him. His genealogy is never recorded, his birth and death never mentioned, and his priesthood never transferred. Melchizedek is a mysterious character for most Christians, but the Hebrews knew exactly why the author brought him up. Melchizedek provides a category for understanding a priesthood different from the Levites—one unlimited by ancestry or mortality, and one that did not serve in Israel's earthly sanctuary.

Psalm 110:4, which the audience knew well, makes the connection: "You are a priest forever after the order of Melchizedek." Hebrews explains that Messiah became priest "not on the basis of a legal requirement concerning descent, but by the power of an indestructible life" (Hebrews 7:16). In other words, his priesthood is not tied to Levite genealogy. Like the Levites, the Messiah is a priest. But unlike the Levites, who died and had to be replaced generation after generation, the Messiah's priesthood never ends. It never passes to another because he has been resurrected. He is eternally purified, and doesn't need to offer more sacrifices to deal with his own ritual impurities. Having already passed through death into eternal life, he entered into his priestly service "once for all" (Hebrews 7:27).

"Once for all" doesn't mean, *Jesus is here, so the Levites are finished.*

It means that his priesthood is perpetual. He does not need to renew his tenure or pass it on to another. The Levites continue their ministry on earth, and Jesus never usurps or invalidates it. Like Melchizedek, he belongs to a different priestly order entirely—one perfectly suited for the heavenly temple. He is a different priest for a different temple, the very temple the Hebrews longed to enter in the age to come.

Some assume that when Jesus called his body a temple (John 2:19–21), he was declaring the physical one obsolete. But that's not what he said—or what his audience understood. He was identifying himself as the living meeting place between heaven and earth—the reality the temple had always pointed toward. His words heightened its meaning, rather than erasing its role.

Hebrews follows the same pattern. It contrasts the earthly and heavenly sanctuaries not as false and true, but as two connected realities—one reflecting the other. For the Hebrews, this truth was a profound comfort. Even if the Levite priests refused to represent them before God in the earthly temple, they could rest secure in Messiah's priesthood: "We have this as a sure and steadfast anchor of the soul, a hope that enters into the inner place behind the curtain, where Jesus has gone as a forerunner on our behalf, having become a high priest forever after the order of Melchizedek" (Hebrews 6:19).

AN ETERNAL SACRIFICE FOR ETERNAL ATONEMENT

The same concept applies to Jesus's sacrifice. Leviticus teaches that life—found in the blood—makes atonement for sin and impurity, cleansing God's earthly dwelling (Leviticus 17:11). The Levitical rituals did exactly what they were designed to do, no more and no less. Scholar Travis Snow argues that these sacrifices weren't about "getting saved" in the modern Evangelical sense.[45] They never made anyone righteous. Rather, the atonement rituals removed the impurity that human sin and mortality created so God's earthly dwelling would not be violated, and he could remain among his people. Animal sacrifice was effective, but its scope was limited to the earthly realm.

The author of Hebrews builds on this but makes a crucial distinction: Jesus is not a goat or bull. His death was never intended to grant access to the earthly temple—that would contradict the Torah. Likewise, no one believed an animal sacrifice could render someone pure enough to enter God's very presence in the heavenly realm. As Hebrews 10:1 reminds us: "For since the law has but a shadow of the good things to come instead of the true form of these realities, it can never, by the same sacrifices that are continually offered every year, make perfect those who draw near." Animal sacrifices maintained ceremonial purity for the earthly temple, but they could not perfect a person or provide the eternal life required to stand before the Most High God.

Access to the eternal temple—the one that will descend in the age to come—requires a different sacrifice. Jesus's sacrifice meets this need. It atones eternally, making a person pure forever. Like our puppy illustration, the real dog was never a *replacement* for the toy. It answered a different longing. In the same way, Jesus's death was not a replacement for Levitical sacrifices but the answer to a different need: eternal purification for entrance into the eternal temple.

When Messiah entered the heavenly temple, he did so "by means of his own blood, thus securing an eternal redemption" (Hebrews 9:12). Just as animal blood allowed temporary access to God's earthly dwelling, the Messiah's blood secures everlasting access to God himself. The Hebrews did not need to fear that exclusion from the earthly temple meant eternal impurity. For them, Messiah's sacrifice purifies forever: "We have confidence to enter the holy places by the blood of Jesus … since we have a great priest over the house of God … with our hearts sprinkled clean and our bodies washed with pure water" (Hebrews 10:19–22).

EARTHLY LOSS, ETERNAL GAIN

Taken together, the earthly temple, the Levitical priesthood, and animal sacrifices form the backbone of Hebrews' argument. The author does not present these as broken or obsolete. The danger was not returning to them, but losing access to the eternal realities they point to by denying the Messiah.

The Hebrews faced a crisis: should they deny Jesus to avoid persecution and preserve their place in the earthly temple? The author's answer is a firm no. His warning is clear: do not throw away eternity by denying Messiah now. Again and again, the author pleads: *Hold fast.* Their eternal share depends on fidelity to the Messiah. Jesus is their eternal High Priest, ministering in the true heavenly temple—a dwelling they cannot afford to lose. Even if they suffer rejection, exclusion, or loss of access to the earthly temple, their representation before God stands firm, because it rests in Messiah alone.

Near the end of the letter, the author urges them not to grow weary but to lift up their drooping hands and strengthen their weak knees. He reminds them that what's at stake isn't access to a physical place—like Sinai or Jerusalem's temple—but the eternal reality to which those earthly places correspond. To hold on to that hope, they must listen to the voice of their Messiah—"do not refuse him who speaks"—and attend closely to the Torah and the Prophets, which point toward the unshakable kingdom he has secured (Hebrews 12).

The author makes no attempt to soften the truth. To honor the Messiah meant paying a price the audience already knew too well—the scorn of the temple authorities, and likely far worse. To comfort them, he points to the Messiah's own example: Jesus too bore suffering "outside the camp," beyond the city gates. The temple and city they love are precious, but even they will pass away. Their true hope lies in "the city that is yet to come" (Hebrews 13:14). If they lose access to Jerusalem's temple, they're urged to offer "a sacrifice of praise ... the fruit of lips that acknowledge his name," through good deeds and generosity (Hebrews 13:15–16).

Seen in this light, Hebrews does not dismiss Levitical practices. It elevates the temple, sacrifices, and the priesthood as anchors for loyalty to the Messiah, who ministers in the eternal temple. Levitical worship retains value in this age, but inclusion in the age to come rests on allegiance to Jesus. If forced to choose, the author would rather have his audience forfeit the earthly temple than deny the one who reigns over the eternal.

FINAL THOUGHTS: SEEING HEBREWS IN CONTEXT

Understanding the pressures faced by early believers helps us to read Hebrews with fresh eyes—and to expose how much our biases can shape interpretation. Too often, we assume that everything in Leviticus is inferior or obsolete because of Jesus.

But Hebrews does not portray the Levitical system as useless. The two are not a placeholder and replacement, one ousting the other. They are different forms of worship, each fitting its own realm and age—the earthly mirroring the heavenly. The Levites and temple sacrifices remain functional in this age. Yet the letter warns that participation in the age to come hinges on allegiance to Messiah in this one. The ultimate hope is not in the rituals themselves, but in the eternal triumph they point toward: the day Yahweh arrives on earth in his glorious, heavenly tent.

The original audience desperately needed this reminder. The letter arrived at the perfect moment. Within a few years, the temple would be destroyed, and the Jewish people would enter the longest season of exile from their holy place—a displacement that continues to this day.

The challenge we face today is not that different from the Hebrews. The Jerusalem believers faced pressure to cling to Levitical practices by denying what Jesus had done. Today, we face the opposite: pressure to deny Levitical practices because of what Jesus has done. Hebrews disarms both. Neither Leviticus nor the Messiah is to be rejected. The letter urges us to hear Scripture rightly, orienting our hearts toward the Messiah in this age as we await the age to come. Confessing Jesus as Messiah will bring opposition, but we must not lose heart, even if we find ourselves "outside the camp" for what we believe.

When Jesus taught his disciples to pray, he gave them words that bridged the very worlds that Hebrews sets before us: "Your kingdom come, your will be done, *on earth as it is in heaven*" (Matthew 6:10). I sometimes imagine the Hebrews whispering those words under their breath as they lingered in the temple corridors, under the Sadducees' watchful eye. Did they pray these words in the midst of the temple when persecution came and they found themselves leaving its courts for the final time, knowing they would never again be able to go back? Did these words comfort them when waiting for Messiah's return became costly?

As we pray the same words today, we have an opportunity to more fully grasp what the Hebrews already knew. The temple, its rituals, its very forms of worship—they are not obsolete. Even in a world currently without a temple, these things matter within their own context because they remind us who Messiah is and what he's doing. To insist that Jesus has replaced them strips Hebrews of its ongoing truth and belittles the Messiah's active ministry in the heavenly tent in this moment. To cast aside Leviticus is, in its own way, to shrink back from our confession today. Like the Hebrews, we face a choice. Will we trust the unseen reality of God's eternal temple? Or deny the Messiah's role by discrediting the earthly reflections of what he is doing?

Hebrews invites us to walk the temple corridors with the first believers—to share in their longing for what is unseen, and to join our hope with theirs in God's eternal story. For too long we have let Hebrews stand in judgment over Leviticus, disqualifying its systems and practices or transforming them into new meanings entirely. But we can read Hebrews differently, in light of the Torah that it rests upon and the testimony of its original audience. Like them, we can recover the harmony between the Messiah and Leviticus.

Just as the Levites tended the earthly temple, our great High Priest prepares the heavenly tent. These two realms of worship have never been in competition. God designed them to mingle in parallel harmony, a gift on the land reminding us of what awaits—the day the two realms intersect. As we wait, the story continues to unfold under the same heavens, with Messiah ministering above and Israel bearing witness below. Our greatest hope rehearsed, *"on earth as it is in heaven,"* until heaven finally comes to earth.

10

THE NEW COVENANT IN
A LEVITICAL LIGHT

COVENANT IS A THEME that runs throughout Scripture, from the promises to Abraham, to the covenant at Sinai, to the new covenant promised in the Prophets. Leviticus, with its detailed instructions on priesthood, sacrifice, and holiness, provided Israel with the covenant framework for life in God's presence. When the New Testament writers speak of the new covenant, they are drawing on this long story, showing how the promises throughout the Scriptures find their fulfillment in the Messiah.

The new covenant lies at the heart of Christian theology, shaping how believers understand God's relationship with humanity. In much of Christian tradition, however, the new covenant is understood as a clean break from the old ways: a relationship with God that is no longer dependent on observing Torah or offering sacrifices. Jesus's sacrifice is seen as the ultimate fulfillment, replacing the need for any Torah observance—especially Levitical rites—while also bringing the indwelling Spirit and the transformation of the human heart, freely available to all who believe in him. For anyone familiar with Reformed teaching, this is nothing new. It's the standard paradigm, covered in most basic theology classes and considered foundational. Yet this interpretation is deeply problematic, for reasons we are beginning to see.

Jesus himself said that he did not come to abolish anything spoken through the Torah or the Prophets—the very foundation of both the old and new covenants. The prophets never expected Leviticus, let alone the covenant itself, to disappear the moment Jesus died on the cross. The earliest believers continued to practice animal sacrifice and Levitical liturgies in faithful submission to the covenant given at Sinai.

Despite the clear continuity in Scripture, the prevailing assumption in much of Christian thought is that the new covenant replaced the old. But the biblical story tells a different tale. The old covenant is woven into the new, its practices and promises still alive within God's covenant with Israel. If we accept the assumption that the old covenant has been canceled, "fulfilled" in Jesus at the cross and thereby disqualifying anything Levitical, we risk missing the deeper purpose of what Jesus truly accomplished. But this raises a crucial question: if the new covenant *doesn't* replace the old, what exactly *does* it do?

I won't provide a lengthy theology of biblical covenants here. (I have saved that deeper dive for the Appendix.) What follows is intended as a concise overview, showing how the main covenants connect and intersect with one another. When viewed in simple terms, it becomes clear that Jesus's death on the cross does not cancel the Mosaic covenant. Rather, the new covenant serves as the means through which all the biblical covenants will ultimately be accomplished. Let's explore how it all works.

GOD'S COVENANT WITH ABRAHAM

Genesis contains the stories of the first covenants in the Bible. A covenant is a sacred agreement, a weighty promise. While the word isn't used specifically until the Noah story, the relationship between God and the first humans could be described as *covenantal*:

- In Genesis 1, God would bless humanity, and they in turn would be fruitful and rule over his creation.

- In Genesis 2, God allowed the man and woman to work and keep the garden in his presence, and they (in theory) would follow his instructions.

- In Genesis 6, God would send a flood to cleanse the land from violence and corruption but Noah's family would be spared and continue to live by God's righteous standards.

The pattern is clear. By the time we get to the story of Abraham, we are already used to the idea that the way God partners with humans to rule his creation is through covenants. In Genesis 15 (and expanded in Genesis 17 and 22) promises Abraham a great name, a great nation, innumerable descendants, divine blessing, and land. This covenant is unconditional: God requires nothing from Abraham. God declares, *"I'll do this. I promise to do these things. I'm the one who's going to make it happen. It's on me."*

I will make you exceedingly fruitful, and I will make nations of you, and kings will come from you. I will establish *My covenant between Me and you and your descendants after you* throughout their generations as *an everlasting covenant,* to be God to you and to your descendants after you. And I will give to you and to your descendants after you *the land where you live as a stranger, all the land of Canaan, as an everlasting possession;* and I will be their God. (Genesis 17:6–8, NASB2020, emphasis added)

Let's note a few key points:

- The recipients: Abraham and his descendants are the ones to whom the promises are made. The promises are directed to a specific person and his family.

- The covenant's term: The covenant is everlasting. These promises are eternal. They never end.

- Any conditions: The covenant is unconditional. God himself will accomplish everything; Abraham's obedience is not required.

Throughout the narrative of Genesis, Abraham sometimes acts righteously. At other times he fails, making choices that put the covenant and its promises in jeopardy. Yet God, because of his commitment to Abraham, often intervenes. Despite Abraham's failures, God remains committed to working through this family to bring about his plans to bless all the families of the world. This same pattern repeats with Abraham's grandson, Jacob, and resonates in the story of his great-grandson Joseph. Across Genesis, God remains steadfastly committed to this covenant family.

GOD'S COVENANT WITH ISRAEL

At Sinai, God expanded the promises that he had already given to Abraham. The land, the name, the blessings, the fruitfulness—all of that remained—but now Israel, Abraham's descendants, inherited something greater: his presence.

Unlike Abraham, who endured famine, hostile neighbors, and displacement, Israel was promised security in the land with God dwelling among them. This gift is unique to the Mosaic covenant. Leviticus laid out the means of hosting that presence—priests, sacrifices, and holiness maintaining God's dwelling in their midst. But this gift was conditional: God promised his presence and blessing in the land, if Israel walked in obedience. God said, "If you agree to do this, I'll agree to do that." Israel agreed to keep the Torah, declaring, "All that Yahweh has spoken, we will do!"

Of course, Israel's enthusiasm is short-lived. Yet their failure never nullified the covenant. Disobedience brought consequences—loss of land, exile, and the withdrawal of God's presence. Still, even in exile, God promised to remember Abraham, restore Israel, bring them back to the land, and reestablish Levitical worship so they could once again host him. This rhythm of faithfulness, failure, judgment, and restoration runs through the story, all pointing toward a final atonement and ultimate renewal. Moses captures this cycle in Deuteronomy 32, confirming that God's covenant endures until he fully atones for his land and his people.

In short, the Mosaic covenant is with Israel, as they are its recipients; and conditional, where safety and blessing in the land are contingent upon Israel's faithfulness.

GOD'S COVENANT WITH DAVID

Later, God makes a covenant with King David, reiterating the promises made to Abraham and Israel while expanding them. He confirms the land and the hosting of his presence, and adds the promise of an eternal throne, kingdom, and king. 1 Chronicles 17:8–15 provides a clear summary:

> And I have been with you wherever you have gone and have cut off all your enemies from before you. And *I will make for you a name, like the name of the great ones of the earth.* And I will appoint *a place for my people Israel and will plant them, that they may dwell in their own place and be disturbed no more ...* When your days are fulfilled to walk with your fathers, *I will raise up your offspring after you,* one of your own sons, and *I will establish his kingdom.* He shall build a house for me, and *I will establish his throne forever. I will be to him a father,* and he shall be to me a son. *I will not take my steadfast love from him ...* but *I will confirm him in my house and in my kingdom forever, and his throne shall be established forever.*

Like Abraham, David's name would be great. Like at Sinai, God's presence would ensure his people's safety. But now, God also promises an eternal king and kingdom to David, resting under Yahweh's favor forever. This king would reign perfectly and eternally over Israel. The Davidic Covenant is made with David and his descendant; is everlasting; and is unconditional. Like with Abraham, God would accomplish the whole thing. He required nothing of David.

Notice that at each turn the covenant expands, but the expansion never negates what came before it. Instead, each iteration adds to the promises for Abraham's family. The blessings promised to Abraham are set in motion at Sinai; the gift of hosting God's presence is solidified under David, who unifies Israel in worship and consecrates a permanent place for God's presence. Each covenant grows in scope and richness, always including the prior promises. God, in his generosity, continually lavishes more goodness upon his people.

To review, we have surveyed three main covenants:

- The Abrahamic covenant: a great name, great nation, blessing, numerous descendants, land.

- The Mosaic covenant: all of the above, plus hosting God's presence in the promised land.

- The Davidic covenant: all of the above, plus an eternal king and kingdom for this land and people.

The Abrahamic and Davidic covenants are unconditional. Abraham and David did nothing to earn or secure what God promised. The Mosaic covenant, by contrast, is conditional. To host God's presence and live securely in the land, Israel must follow God's instructions as expressed in the Torah. At Sinai, Israel agreed to these terms, committing themselves to live by God's commands.

THE NEW COVENANT

Throughout the Prophets—especially Jeremiah and Isaiah—God speaks of a "new covenant." The term *new* can be misleading in English. When we think of something new, we often imagine replacing something old entirely, like tossing an old pair of running shoes for a new pair. This is not what the prophets have in mind.

The covenant is "new" in the sense that it is *different* from the one made with Moses at Sinai. Unlike the Mosaic covenant, which was conditional and vulnerable to human failure, the new covenant, like the Abrahamic and Davidic covenants, is accomplished entirely by God himself. Jeremiah summarizes: "Behold, days are coming," declares the LORD, "when I will make a new covenant with the house of Israel and the house of Judah, not like the covenant which I made with their fathers … which they broke, although I was a husband to them … I will put My [Torah] within them and write it on their heart; and I will be their God, and they shall be My people … for I will forgive their wrongdoing, and their sin I will no longer remember."

In this promise, God fulfills *all* his promises throughout every covenant. A few key points are clear:

- The recipients: The new covenant is with house of Israel and Judah—the family of Abraham and David.

- The covenant's term: The new covenant is everlasting. The covenant's fulfillment comes after a period of time, referred to by Jeremiah as "Jacob's Trouble" (Jeremiah 30:7–8).

- Any conditions: The new covenant is unconditional. God requires nothing of Israel; he himself will accomplish it.

Taken together, the Abrahamic, Mosaic, Davidic, and new covenants form a single story: the everlasting covenant—the everlasting covenant God made with Israel. When viewed progressively, they do not cancel each other; they build on one another. Within Jewish tradition—the people to whom the covenant actually belongs—the "new" covenant is not a rejection of Sinai but a renewal, a strengthening of what came before. Covenants do not cancel each other out with each new iteration. Paul alludes to this principle in Galatians 3:15: "even with a man-made covenant, no one annuls it or adds to it once it has been ratified."

In other words, expansions never void earlier promises. God's covenants with Abraham and David were unconditional. The covenant at Sinai, however, was conditional. Israel broke it again and again. That failure created a dilemma: God had promised land, blessing, a great name, and his presence—but Israel couldn't keep their end of the bargain. So what should God do? Change the Torah? Lower the standard of righteousness? Cancel Israel's covenant and choose another people to start over with? Of course not. God's promises cannot change. His standards cannot change. His Torah cannot change, but he *can* change Israel. They are his creatures; they can be re-created.

This is the heart of the new covenant. God did not scrap the Torah or replace Israel with another people. He needed to address Israel's inability to keep their promise. Instead of nullifying the Torah, handing the promises to someone else, or inventing a new system to save them (cue Replacement Theology), he strengthened his covenant with Israel so that its fulfillment would depend not on their faithfulness, but on his.

The Torah would remain the righteous standard for his people. Inscribed upon their hearts, it becomes the very beating heart of the new covenant, animated by God's own Spirit. And all their past failures—the generations of egregious sin, all the broken promises? God would just forgive them. He would wipe the slate clean and overlook their transgressions. God can do that. He is rich in compassion, full of mercy. Rather than letting his promises to bless the nations fail, he would uphold both ends of the covenant himself—and guarantee it with his own blood.

JESUS AND THE NEW COVENANT

Jesus cut this new, everlasting covenant with his blood at his death. During the Passover meal the night before, Jesus explains:

> Now as they were eating, Jesus took bread, and after blessing it broke it and gave it to the disciples, and said, "Take, eat; this is my body." And he took a cup, and when he had given thanks he gave it to them, saying, "Drink of it, all of you, for this is my blood of the [new] covenant, which is poured out for many for the forgiveness of sins. (Matthew 26:26–28)

Compare this with Jeremiah 31 and notice the parallel language: "I will make a new covenant with the house of Israel and the house of Judah … for I will forgive their wrongdoing, and their sin I will no longer remember." Jesus fully understood the messianic implications of Jeremiah's words. In the hours before his crucifixion, he announced that his blood secured covenantal forgiveness for his nation. Jesus did not explain his death as a blanket provision of forgiveness for all human sin. He knew the Prophets. He knew Jeremiah. The covenant in his blood has a specific recipient and purpose: his blood sealed the new covenant with Israel, ensuring the future restoration God has planned for them. Jesus would accomplish for Israel what they could not achieve on their own.

Zechariah, a relative of Jesus, prophesied the same truth at the birth of his son, John the Baptist. His prayer is saturated with the language of covenant and promise:

> Blessed be the Lord God *of Israel*,
>> for he has *visited* and *redeemed his people*
>> and has raised up a horn of salvation *for us*
>> in the *house of his servant David*,
>> as he spoke by the mouth of his *holy prophets* from of old,
>> to show the *mercy promised to our fathers*

and to remember his *holy covenant,*
the *oath he swore* to our father *Abraham,*
to grant us that we, being delivered from our enemies,
might serve him without fear,
in holiness and righteousness before him all our days.

(Luke 1:68–75, emphasis added)

Zechariah's prayer ties every covenant together into one unified expectation: that God would act decisively to redeem Israel. The birth of his son moved him to proclaim God's promise to restore his people to holiness—the very theme at the heart of Leviticus.[46] When Paul referred to this new covenant, he too anticipated a future fulfillment of the promises secured at the cross:

> In the same way also he took the cup, after supper, saying, "This cup is the new covenant in my blood. Do this, as often as you drink it, in remembrance of me." For as often as you eat this bread and drink the cup, *you proclaim Lord's death until he comes.* (1 Corinthians 11:25–26)

To proclaim the Lord's death until he comes is to proclaim what his death accomplished. By his blood on the cross, the new covenant was secured for Israel—a covenant enabling them to live faithfully by God's standards (something the Corinthians were failing to do in their meals together, which is why Paul raises the issue). But proclaiming the Messiah's death *until he comes* also looks forward in hope: Paul expects the Lord to return in glory and bring the covenant to its fullness. Every promise God made to Abraham's family is on the way.

Jesus knew this. Zechariah believed it. Paul taught it. Each year, when the first followers of Jesus celebrated the Passover, the bread and cup reminded them of the flesh he offered and the blood he shed to cut the everlasting covenant with Yahweh.

Few believers realize that *this* is what they are proclaiming when they participate in communion. When I first took the bread and cup, I thought it was a reminder of what Jesus did for me personally—how he forgave my sin and died in my place. I thought that was what the new covenant was all about. But that is not its focus. The new covenant is not with me personally, nor with Christians in general. The new covenant exists to enable God to finally give Israel all the promises, because his covenant people will finally live as he desires.

HEBREWS AND THE "BETTER" COVENANT

The author of Hebrews shares the same hope as the prophets and apostles: God has not scrapped his Torah or his people. Yet he describes the new covenant as *better*. That single word has fueled centuries of interpretation. Many commentaries assume that *better* means the Mosaic covenant is inferior or temporary, "passing away," with the temple's destruction in 70 CE as proof. Here's the key text:

> But as it is, [the Messiah] has obtained a ministry that is as much more excellent than the old as the covenant he mediates is better, since it is enacted on better promises. For if that first covenant had been faultless, there would have been no occasion to look for a second … In speaking of a new covenant, he makes the first obsolete. And what is becoming obsolete and growing old is ready to vanish away. (Hebrews 8:6–7,13)

Read quickly, it sounds like the Torah itself is vanishing. But pause and read carefully. The writer never says the Torah is passing away. What is "growing old" is not Levitical worship, the temple, or the sacrifices—but the *first covenant* itself.

The first covenant is not the Torah—it is Israel's agreement to keep the Torah. Israel's failure to uphold that agreement, not God's standard, is the problem. God values his Torah so highly that when he re-creates his people, he will write it directly on their hearts, empowering them to live faithfully. The issue has never been God's standards, but Israel's inability to fulfill their covenantal commitment.

So why is the new covenant better? Hebrews gives the answer: *it is enacted on better promises.* The Mosaic covenant rested on Israel's ability to obey. The new covenant rests on God's ability to re-create his people. Where Israel failed, God takes both sides of the covenant into his own hands. That is the "better promise"—not lower standards, but stronger guarantees.

"If that first covenant had been faultless," Hebrews explains, "there would have been no occasion to look for a second" (8:7). The fault lay in Israel, not the covenant itself. Had they kept it, the blessings of land, security, and God's presence would have flourished. But they didn't. God's plans, however, cannot be thwarted by an unfaithful partner. This is what makes the new covenant better: it is founded not on Israel's ability to keep their promise, but on God's ability to keep his.

As humans, Israel fell short. In Hebrews 8, what is passing away is not the Torah; what is passing away is Israel's inability to keep it. Israel couldn't do it. Christians can't either. No one can. History shows we try and fail, repeatedly. We need to be re-created. The new covenant, mediated by Messiah, guarantees that re-creation. Hebrews puts it this way: "When [the Messiah] appeared as a high priest of the good things that have come ... he entered once for all into the holy places, by means of his own blood, thus securing an eternal redemption ... Therefore he is the mediator of a new covenant, so that those who are called may receive the promised eternal inheritance" (Hebrews 9:11–15).

In the mind of Hebrews, the Messiah secures God's promises by rescuing Israel from the consequences of their broken word. Breaking the Mosaic covenant brought a cycle of exile, suffering, and death outside the land. But God would not abandon his people to the grave—or abandon his righteous standards.

Through the Messiah, he created a new and better covenant for a new and better world, where every promise to Israel and the nations will be fulfilled. With it come new hearts, animated by the Spirit of God. On those hearts the Torah will shine from within, enabling Israel to live by God's instructions, reflect his image, and host his presence without failure.

GENTILES AND THE NEW COVENANT

It can feel disorienting to realize that the new covenant is first and foremost with Israel. Evangelicals aren't used to seeing ourselves as "outsiders" in the biblical story, grafted into what was never ours by birthright. But this is not a threat. Being invited into Israel's covenant is to share in promises far greater than anything we could claim apart from them.

God's promise to Abraham always included the nations (a reality that the earliest believers experienced in radical ways). He chose one family not at the expense of the many, but for the blessing of the many. By grace, Gentiles are brought into this everlasting covenant through faith in the work of its mediator, Jesus the Messiah (Hebrews 7:22).

When we talk about "faith in Jesus," we often reduce it to believing certain facts about him—that he lived, died, rose again, and bore our sins. These truths are precious, but Scripture goes deeper. Gentiles are joined not merely by faith in those events, but by trusting the very work Jesus carried out as Israel's mediator. Paul explains that Gentiles are adopted into God's family, made co-heirs of its blessings, and destined to share in the inheritance of the world to come—if, like Abraham, we trust God's promises (Romans 8:14–17, Colossians 3:24, Ephesians 1:3–14; 3:6). The Spirit's indwelling is the downpayment of that hope, proof that our faith is not in vain (Ephesians 1:14). Already our hearts are being transformed, as we await the day that work is complete.

But we must remember: the new covenant does not belong to Christians. It is God's gift to Israel, so they can remain faithful to him. Gentile believers rejoice not because we replace Israel, but because we are invited to share in their blessing. As God promised Abraham, "In you, all nations will be blessed."

This is why, in our family, when we commemorate the Lord's Table or celebrate Passover in the spring, we give thanks. We are not Jewish—and that's okay. Ethnicity is not what secures our place before God; faith in his promises, expressed through obedience to his standards, is what matters (Galatians 5:6, 1 Corinthians 7:17–20). Still, we remember that by birth we remain outsiders, sons and daughters according to the promise, not the flesh. Our assurance rests in God's covenant faithfulness to Israel. If he has not forgotten them, he will not forget us.

So we lift the cup with joy. From Abraham's family, the tribe of Judah, the line of David, God raised up a servant for his people. Messiah was faithful to them at the cross, and he will be faithful to them at his return. Through him, the covenant promises are secure—for Israel, and for all who share in their blessing. That is our hope for the restoration of all things. "Let us hold fast the confession of our hope without wavering, for he who promised is faithful" (Hebrews 10:23).

FINAL THOUGHTS

When read within its plain context, many common Christian assumptions about the new covenant simply fall apart. Arguments that claim that the new covenant frees us from obeying the Torah, or that Leviticus was replaced, overlook the covenant's actual promise: the Torah will dwell eternally within the human heart. *"I will put my [Torah] in their minds and write it on their hearts. I will be their God, and they will be my people."*

It is hard to be "set free" from something God has promised to place inside you. Gentiles, after all, were never bound to the same covenantal obligations as Israel—but they were always part of God's plan to bless the nations through Israel's faithfulness.

The claim that new covenant belongs only to Christians—and that it releases God from his obligation to fulfill his promises to Abraham's family—twists Scripture beyond recognition. I reached a point in my own journey where I could no longer accept that view. I needed to understand the new covenant in a way that honored the Torah, upheld the ongoing authority Jesus gave to Leviticus, and respected the Jewish people to whom these promises were first given.

Through the new covenant, God's promises come to fruition. The Torah, written on renewed hearts, guides his people into everlasting peace and life in his presence. This is not a different Torah or a lighter set of rules, but the same standard, empowered by God's Spirit. By grace, the nations are invited to share in this blessing through faith. As God told Abraham, "In you, all nations will be blessed." Gentiles too are "sprinkled clean" by the Messiah, purified to draw near to the God of creation, and welcomed into his family. As image-bearers, Gentiles bring a unique and vital contribution to God's multiethnic family—a contribution that God's promises to Israel have always celebrated.

We serve a mighty, risen Master whose Spirit already regenerates the hearts of his people. Yet if we hope for our own resurrection, for a world free from death and suffering, and for life in God's glorious presence, then we must also hope for the fullness of the covenant God made with Israel. That hope rests not on their faithfulness, but on God's.

For many of us, this is a paradigm shift. It doesn't ask us to believe only in *our* salvation—it asks us to believe in *theirs*. "Only if the heavens above can be measured, and the foundations of the earth below be searched out, will I reject all the descendants of Israel because of all they have done" (Jeremiah 31:37).

God's promises to Israel are unshakable, and in them we find our hope. To hope in Messiah is to hope in the God who will bring his covenant people—and through them, all nations—to their destined glory. Through a covenantal connection, we join ourselves to Israel's Messiah, heirs of the same hope, trusting in the God who never breaks his word.

11

WHY DON'T WE HAVE A TEMPLE?

AS WE'VE WORKED OUR WAY through the idea that Jesus cancels out everything in Leviticus, it's become clear that many of our assumptions clash with Scripture. When you step into the worldview of Jesus and the biblical authors, Leviticus doesn't shrink into the background. It stands there, shoulder to shoulder, right alongside our hope in the Messiah and in God's enduring promises. But this realization also raises practical questions. If Jesus doesn't replace Leviticus, what are we supposed to do with the fact that there is no temple in Jerusalem? How are we meant to think about sacrifices, God's holiness, and Israel's calling when so much of Leviticus feels lost to history? Has God's plan shifted? Or does its expression look different right now?

I circled around these questions for a long time myself. Over coffee one morning while I was still brainstorming ideas for this book, my husband cut right to the chase: *If Levitical worship is still so important to God, why isn't it happening today? Aren't believers the temple now? And if not ... what are we supposed to do—start raising goats in the backyard?*

He wasn't actually serious about raising or sacrificing animals. I mean, aside from the obvious fact that we're not Levite priests, God never handed out "DIY altar kits" for backyard use. But his questions were real. If Jesus doesn't replace Leviticus, and if God isn't finished with the Mosaic covenant, then where exactly does that leave us?

For many, the current geopolitical reality seems to settle the matter. It feels like proof that Levitical worship belongs to the past. But the Bible's story isn't so quick to move on. There is one more thread in the conversation of Leviticus that we must not overlook—the place where that worship belongs. For Leviticus to matter, the temple must matter. And for the temple to matter, the land beneath it must matter. The story of God's presence is not just spiritual. It's rooted in real soil, on a mountain he chose, in a land he married (Isaiah 62:4).

The moment we speak about the temple or the modern land of Israel, we might feel like we're talking about matters of politics, unrelated to faith. But Scripture's concern arises from another place—not from geopolitics, but from God's covenant purposes. The tension we feel isn't between faith and politics, but between eternity's story and our own social location.

Many of us have inherited a faith that reveres heaven but neglects earth. Yet Scripture ties holiness not only to our hearts, but to the land. The temple and the land of Israel are not political symbols, but sacred ground in God's plan of restoration. Leviticus draws our gaze back to the temple—its purpose, its place in God's plan, and what true worship looks like when the temple stands beyond reach.

JESUS LAMENTS THE COVENANT CONSEQUENCES

The temple didn't disappear by random chance. The absence of Levitical worship today isn't an accident. To understand why, we can look to Jesus himself. He stood over Jerusalem and wept, speaking the very warnings the Torah had clearly spelled out. Through his grief, we see that God was doing something intentional—even in the devastation.

Near the end of Matthew, Jesus condemns the religious elite of his day and predicts the fall of the temple. It's a well-known lament:

> "O Jerusalem, Jerusalem, the city that kills the prophets and stones those who are sent to it! How often would I have gathered your children together as a hen gathers her brood under her wings, and you were not willing! See, your house is left to you desolate. For I tell you, you will not see me again, until you say, 'Blessed is he who comes in the name of the Lord.'" Jesus left the temple and was going away, when his disciples came to point out to him the buildings of the temple. But he answered them, "You see all these, do you not? Truly, I say to you, there will not be left here one stone upon another that will not be thrown down." (Matthew 23:37–24:2)

The severity of these words echo warnings far older. The covenant consequences we read about in the Torah were knocking on the door of Israel's leadership in Jesus's day. In his lament, Jesus is not merely fast-forwarding time to foresee the temple's downfall forty years later. He is grieving over the covenant rupture already unfolding before him, a pattern of consequence replaying what Moses had warned of more than a thousand years earlier:

> But if you will not listen to me and will not do all these commandments, if you spurn my statutes … then I will do this to you: I will visit you with panic, with wasting disease and fever that consume the eyes and make the heart ache. And you shall sow your seed in vain, for your enemies shall eat it. I will set my face against you, and you shall be

struck down before your enemies. Those who hate you shall rule over you, and you shall flee when none pursues you. (Leviticus 26:14–17)

If Israel was faithful, God's blessings would follow, and his presence would assure prosperity and safety. If they were unfaithful, God would hand them over to their enemies. Jesus wept, seeing not only the city's coming ruin but the deeper wound beneath it—covenant unfaithfulness. In the verses preceding, he pronounces seven woes over the religious rulers, echoing the grievances listed in Leviticus 26 and Deuteronomy 28.

By Jesus's day, Israel's leadership had perverted justice and killed the prophets that God had sent to warn them. The chief priests, elders, and scribes were charged with maintaining covenant fidelity on a national level. Jesus was both angry and deeply grieved over their failures. Because God's character requires him to uphold his covenant, Jesus knew that Israel would face the consequences of their hardened hearts. We can feel the pain in the words of our Master. He desperately wanted to gather his people as their Messiah during his earthly ministry, but they were unwilling. It broke his heart.

And when he drew near and saw the city, he wept over it, saying, "Would that you, even you, had known on this day the things that make for peace! But now they are hidden from your eyes. For the days will come upon you, when your enemies will set up a barricade around you, surround you, and hem you in on every side, and tear you down to the ground, you and your children within you. And they will not leave one stone upon another in you, because you did not know the time of your visitation." (Luke 19:41–44)

My eyes sting just reading it. Picture Jesus pausing on the hillside, the city stretched out before him—Jerusalem, the place where heaven once touched earth, the home of God's own presence. He looks out over its crowded streets, its shining stones, and knows what's coming. He knows that the people he loves are walking straight into the consequences of their choices. He knows the prophecies, every line of warning from the Torah. And in that moment, the weight of it all breaks over him. He's absolutely wrecked.

THE PATTERN OF WORSHIP

What's striking about this scene is what Jesus doesn't say. When he weeps over Jerusalem, he never once points to himself as the reason. There's no mention of his sacrificial death, no talk of the new covenant in his blood. He doesn't imply, "Since you've rejected me, the temple's coming down and Leviticus is canceled because I'm the ultimate sacrifice." Instead, he points right back to the Mosaic covenant.

Jesus knew the story. He knew all that the Prophets had spoken. The warnings in the Torah were clear: if Israel turned from God, judgment would follow. What awaited Jerusalem wasn't some brand-new twist in the plan. It was the same pattern playing out again.

The pattern goes something like this:

- Humans dwell with God, at peace, worshipping his presence.

- Humans fail, sin, or rebel.

- God exiles humans from his presence, and they face the consequences of their choices. (For Israel, these consequences are spelled out in advance throughout the Torah.)

- In his mercy and in accordance with his covenant promises, God allows humans to return to proximity with him (see Leviticus 26:44–45, Deuteronomy 30:1–3).

- Humans rebuild an altar.

- Humans resume temple-style worship, hosting God's presence once again—though always outside of the Edenic ideal.

From Eden onward, the pattern repeats: humans dwell with God, fail, face exile, and eventually restore worship anew at the altar again—Adam and Eve, Cain, Abel, and Seth, Noah and his sons, each recycling the same pattern of ruin and restoration. And this is just the warmup. When we get to Israel as a nation, the cycles unfold on a much larger scale. After Joshua leads them into the land, Levitical worship becomes corrupted and distorted. Judges tells a story of not only brutal battles with neighboring nations, but horrifying internal strife. Then David steps in, unites the tribes, restores worship, and dedicates the holy place. Solomon builds the temple—a shining, if brief, golden era.

But the cycle of covenant failure spirals again. Later kings let the people down, leaving Israel exposed to Assyrian and Babylonian invasions. The Babylonian exile leaves a traumatic scar that the biblical authors never forget. Yet even here, God's mercy shows up. Ezra and Nehemiah record the story of Israel's return to the land: Levitical worship resumes, the temple and city walls are rebuilt—though never quite the same as before. Over the centuries, Israel faces repeated invasions and occupations. The temple is defiled, sacrifices are interrupted, worship comes to a halt … and then, often miraculously, the temple is cleansed and sacrifices restored.

Through it all, the cycle repeats: worship, failure, exile, return. And through it all, God's presence remains, patiently working through history and human hearts to keep the covenant alive.

THE ONGOING ROLE OF THE MOSAIC COVENANT

It is striking that many Christians point to the absence of a Jerusalem temple as "proof" that the Mosaic covenant has been canceled. Yet Jesus drew the opposite conclusion. If God were finished with the temple, the priests, the people, and the sacrifices, then he would also be finished with the covenant itself. But the covenant cannot be parceled out. It is progressive: new expansions do not erase earlier promises. Either God's covenant is entirely intact and he is faithful to it, or it's not and God is a liar. Why would God still enforce covenant consequences if he considered it void or replaced by some other covenant?

The evidence is compelling. In Jesus's day, Israel hosted God's presence in the earthly temple. Israel's leadership repeatedly failed, something Jesus often pointed out. Within a century, judgment came. The Jewish people were exiled, scattered, and endured nearly two thousand years of suffering, exactly as Deuteronomy 32 warned. Yet, in mercy, God regathered his people.

In 1948 Israel miraculously returned to its land, revived its ancient language, and continues to endure against overwhelming odds. Today, Israel stands in the fading shadow of a recent war. Violent Jew-hate has erupted across the world—unprecedented in my lifetime and spreading fastest among the young. Within the Church, a quieter form of that same hostility lurks, fed by the old belief that the Church has replaced Israel. Among the rising generation of Evangelicals, love for the Jewish people can no longer be taken for granted.[47] Yet, despite relentless opposition, the Jewish people persist.

One vivid sign of covenant expectation is the work of the Temple Institute in Jerusalem, a Jewish non-profit dedicated to rebuilding the temple. Their mission centers on "restoring Temple consciousness" and reawakening the "forgotten commandments" related to worship on Mount Moriah. Through education, research, and physical preparation, they aim to help bring the Holy Temple back into reality.[48] Their stated mission:

> The Temple Institute is dedicated to all aspects of the Divine commandment for Israel to build a house for G-d's presence, the Holy Temple, on Mount Moriah in Jerusalem. The range of the Institute's involvement includes education, research, activism, and actual preparation. Our goal is firstly, to restore Temple consciousness and reactivate these 'forgotten' commandments. We hope that by doing our part, we can participate in the process that will lead to the Holy Temple becoming a reality once more.[49]

Despite significant international and political obstacles, the organization has undertaken monumental steps: pre-approving stones for an altar, verifying the genealogy of Levites qualified to serve as priests, and importing several red heifers in preparation for altar consecration. Regarding the resumption of Levitical worship, they note: "The Temple Institute will wait for as long as it takes. The time for the building of the Temple certainly isn't up to us."[50]

If the covenant had been abolished at the cross, none of this persistence—or Israel's very survival—would make sense. God would have no reason to uphold its terms. Some argue we are in a "Church Age," where God has set Israel aside and now works solely through the church. But this reduces two millennia of Jewish suffering, survival, and restoration to geopolitical accident. Deuteronomy 32 rebukes such thinking: God would not allow Israel's destruction, lest enemies boast, "Our hand is triumphant; it was not the LORD who did this."

The cessation of Jewish worship today, then, is exactly what Jesus lamented: Israel's unfaithfulness brought judgment. The destruction of the temple in 70 CE, centuries of exile, the miraculous return in 1948, and the present longing to resume Levitical worship—all testify to the covenant's endurance. Modern Israel is following the biblically established pattern precisely.

This present reality raises a hard tension when it comes to modern Israel and the Jewish people. As followers of Jesus, we are asked to consider what it means to stand with Israel. For some, compassion for Israel feels like indifference to Palestinian suffering. But that is a false choice. Matt Davis, a Jewish follower of Jesus and host of a popular podcast, puts it this way: "You can grieve innocent loss and pray for mercy on all sides, and you can still believe that God's covenant with Israel still stands. Compassion and covenant are not enemies."[51]

To stand with Israel means committing ourselves to God's purposes for his chosen people, regardless of the present state of their nation or their hearts.[52] It does not require endorsing every government policy or action. Scripture calls us to something deeper than politics: to honor

God's unbreakable promises, to cherish the people through whom he gave us the Messiah, and to hope for the day those promises reach their fullness. If we believe the gospel that Jesus preached, our task is to reflect that same message today: calling Israel to covenantal faithfulness, even when their leadership is imperfect or their actions are controversial. This distinction—between covenantal connection and political endorsement—keeps us anchored in the promises of God rather than in the shifting winds of politics.

RECOVERING A HIGH VIEW OF THE TEMPLE

At the time of this writing, there is no Jewish temple in Jerusalem. For many Western believers, that feels unsurprising. The temple is not part of our cultural or spiritual imagination. Christianity has long treated it with ambivalence—viewing it as outdated, symbolic, or even irrelevant. Many Jews also see it as an antiquated system of worship (and do not desire to see a temple rebuilt).

But who, exactly, decided it was antiquated? Not Scripture. The idea that temple worship has been outgrown or transcended comes from later adaptations, not from the Bible itself. Those conclusions reveal less about God's intent and more about how low our view of his design has become. This is not to diminish or invalidate modern expressions of worship—they are full of devotion and meaning—but to expose how easily we have come to revere the architecture of our own worship patterns while forgetting the one God designed. Our later traditions are beautiful reflections of the longing of God's people to worship him when a temple was no longer standing. But they did not arise because God thought the system he commanded was in need of updating. They arose because the people who loved him were finding ways to honor him in exile.

The temple is iconic in Scripture. Half of the Torah is devoted to tabernacle construction, Levitical service, and the rhythms of sacrificial worship. In biblical language, "worshipping the Lord" almost always means practicing Leviticus—sacrifices, offerings, purification rites, and festival gatherings. The examples are vivid. Hannah traveled annually to

Shiloh to offer sacrifices before pleading for a son (1 Samuel 1). David, longing for God's presence, ordered sacrifices every six steps as the ark was brought to Jerusalem (2 Samuel 6). Jeroboam so feared losing his people to temple worship in Jerusalem that he built rival shrines with golden calves and priests of his own (1 Kings 12). The Psalms celebrate the house of the Lord, and the prophets envision the nations streaming to the temple to learn Torah (Isaiah 2, Zechariah 14). Even in the New Testament, the temple remains central—Jesus taught there, prayed there, and wept over its future destruction.

For a long time, I treated the temple like background scenery in Bible stories. But it wasn't. It was the house of God's presence. Its collapse was devastating for Jews and for the first followers of Jesus. This book rests on the conviction that Leviticus matters. But if Leviticus matters, then the temple—or at least the rituals it prescribes—must matter too. Which raises the questions: If there is no temple, what becomes of Levitical worship? How do its principles carry forward when the holy space is gone, and what does that mean for non-Jews, who were never permitted inside?

The good news is that Scripture anticipates these very questions. Time and again, the Bible shows us how God's people can worship when access to the temple is cut off. The pattern is clear: Levitical principles are not bound to bricks and mortar, nor do they vanish when covenant consequences cause a pause in Jewish worship. They continue to shape worship for Jew and Gentile alike—even when the temple itself is out of reach.

FAITHFUL JEWISH WORSHIP WITHOUT A TEMPLE

When the tabernacle was first constructed, Moses had a problem. He couldn't enter the tent. If he did, he'd contaminate the whole thing. So God handed him Leviticus, a detailed set of instructions and rituals designed to keep his dwelling pure, even in the messy presence of imperfect humans. The stories of Levitical service show both shining moments and glaring failures. Israel struggled with the weighty task of hosting God's presence. Over time, their leaders grew unfaithful, and things unraveled so badly that God had to invoke the covenant consequences. Assyria overtook Israel. Later, Babylon destroyed Jerusalem and the temple, hauling God's people off into exile.

Among those exiled was Daniel. Daniel was well-educated and well-bred, hauled off to Babylon as a teenager (Daniel 1:3–4). As a captive, he was probably separated from his family. He didn't speak the language. Everything was foreign. For three years he studied Chaldean literature, a shocking departure from the Hebraic scrolls he was used to. At times it probably felt like he was completely cut off from his people and his God. Despite the hardship he faced, Daniel did not abandon his Jewish ways. Both God and man honored him for it.

Daniel never made it back home. But he maintained Jewish devotion to God in exile throughout his life, and God was so pleased with Daniel that an angel called him "highly esteemed." Esther and Mordecai, similarly, led the Jewish people in fasting and prayer, refusing to abandon worship, even though the Levitical rituals were impossible in Persia. And we can be fairly certain that they weren't alone—countless faithful exiles throughout history have done the same.

In modern Judaism, Daniel and Esther's examples provide the model for Jewish worship in the absence of temple rituals. Modern Jews pray, fast, and do acts of charity in their communities and synagogues as a spiritual form of Levitical worship. The rabbis leaned heavily on the verse from Hosea 14:2, which the prophet Hosea wrote during a time when temple access was cut off:

> Return, Israel, to the LORD your God,
> > For you have stumbled because of your wrongdoing.
> Take words with you and return to the LORD.
> Say to Him, "Take away all guilt
> > And receive us graciously,
> > So that we may present the bulls of our lips.

That last line—"the bulls of our lips"—sounds awkward in English. Different translations try to clarify: the KJV says calves, the ESV bulls, others render it as *fruit* or *praise*. Hosea's point is that words—prayers, praise, contrition—can stand in for literal sacrifices when the altar isn't available. The author of Hebrews echoes this teaching, urging Jewish believers in his day—likely barred from temple access—to offer the same kind of heartfelt worship: "Through Him then, let's continually offer up a *sacrifice of praise to God,* that is, *the fruit of lips* praising His name. Do not neglect to do good and to share what you have, *for such sacrifices are pleasing to God.*" (Hebrews 13:15–16, emphasis added).

A modern example brings this to life. Joshua Aaron is an Israeli-American musician and follower of Yeshua. He lives in both the U.S. and Israel, traveling the world leading a ministry called Gather the Nations.[53] Years ago, his family made *aliyha*, the process of ethnic Jews returning to live as citizens within Israel. Every time Joshua returns to Israel from abroad, his first stop is often the Western Wall in Jerusalem. He ritually washes his hands, prays, sings, and worships with his family at the crumbling stones.

What's interesting is that he could do these things anywhere. It's not as though he doesn't worship or pray in other places. But his heart is clearly drawn to God's dwelling place in Jerusalem. He is a modern-day fulfillment of Hosea's vision: a faithful Jew returning to the house of the Lord, offering a sacrifice of praise whenever possible. Joshua and his family practice Levitical-style worship as much as circumstances allow, honoring God and Yeshua the Messiah alike.

Stories like these shine as testimonies. God has always desired sincere hearts behind offerings—but that doesn't erase the importance of obedience to his instructions in Leviticus. Ideally, worshippers would offer both sacrifice and sincerity in their hearts. Yet throughout history, when Levitical worship and temple access are impossible, prayer, repentance, generosity, and thanksgiving continue as appropriate offerings for Israel to present. And this tradition continues within Judaism today.

GENTILE WORSHIP, LEVITICAL-STYLE

Levitical rituals were given specifically for the Jewish people. At no point could Gentiles just wander into the inner courts of the temple or start offering sacrifices themselves. Still, the wisdom behind these practices—how to honor God with your life, your resources, and your devotion—applies to anyone who fears God. And the Bible gives us some fantastic examples of Gentiles doing exactly that.

Take Ruth, Rahab, Jethro, and even the Queen of Sheba. These non-Jews risked reputation, comfort, and resources to honor God and protect his people. They often stepped into risky situations to stand alongside the Jewish people. In the New Testament, Cornelius, the Roman centurion we meet in Acts, is another incredible case. He lived in Italy, far from Jerusalem, yet he prayed facing the city and generously gave to the Jewish community. God was so pleased with his Levitical-style devotion that, like Daniel, God sent an angel to interrupt his prayer and announce, "Your prayers and your alms have ascended as a memorial before God" (Acts 10:4). Cornelius's worship literally rose to God like the smoke from a sacrifice.

Even the Magi, pagan sages from the East, demonstrate this kind of Levitical devotion. Matthew tells us that they studied the Jewish Scriptures and watched the heavens for the promised king. When the sign appeared, they crossed deserts and borders to find him, carrying treasures at great personal cost. They had no access to the temple or its altar, yet they offered what they could: worship marked by study, sacrifice, and generosity. Their devotion cost them something—just as every true offering does.

These stories are given for our instruction. They show us that Gentiles can engage in Levitical-style worship—surrendering what's most precious in ways that are faithful and pleasing to God. Even outside the temple, even without priests and an altar, their worship rose to Yahweh, echoing the ancient patterns of devotion that Leviticus laid down.

SPIRITUAL WORSHIP IN THE DIASPORA AND THE TEMPLE OF BELIEVERS TODAY

It makes sense that the apostles encouraged Jesus-following communities scattered throughout the diaspora to adopt a spiritual form of worship. They weren't inventing anything new. The idea of offering spiritual sacrifices through prayer, fasting, and acts of charity already had a long pedigree in Jewish practice. The apostles simply affirmed that this approach worked for both Jews and Gentiles, whether or not anyone had access to a physical temple.

The apostles put it plainly:

- Romans 12:1: "Therefore I urge you, brothers and sisters, by the mercies of God, to present your bodies as a living and holy sacrifice, acceptable to God, which is your spiritual service of worship."

- Ephesians 5:2: "Walk in love, as Christ loved us and gave himself up, a fragrant offering and sacrifice to God."

- Philippians 4:18: "I have received full payment … your gifts have been a fragrant offering, a sacrifice acceptable and pleasing to God."

- 1 Peter 2:5: "Offer spiritual sacrifices that are acceptable to God through Jesus Christ."

- Hebrews 13:15–16: "Through Him then, let's continually offer up a sacrifice of praise … And do not neglect doing good and sharing, for with such sacrifices God is pleased."

Notice how similar the language is to Levitical sacrifices? That's not a coincidence. Even if the temple was standing, these early communities (often a mix of Jews and Gentiles) were treated as expressions of God's presence too. Worship could happen anywhere because God's presence isn't limited to a building.

It's easy for us today, living in an individualistic culture, to read these passages and think, "I am God's temple. The Spirit dwells in me personally." That's true, but it misses the communal worldview the apostles spoke into. The Bible shows that when Jews and Gentiles come together in Messiah, distinct but united in love and laying down divisions, they become a holy dwelling place for God:

- 1 Corinthians 3:16: "Do [you all] not know that you are [all] God's temple and that God's Spirit dwells in you [all]?"

- Ephesians 2:19–22: "You [Gentiles] are fellow citizens with the [Israel] … built on the foundation of the apostles and prophets, [Messiah] Jesus himself being the cornerstone, in whom the whole structure … grows into a holy temple in the Lord."

- 1 Peter 2:5: "You [all] yourselves like living stones are being built up as a spiritual house, to offer spiritual sacrifices acceptable to God through Jesus Christ."

Neither the "temple of all believers" nor the temple of Jesus's body stands as a replacement for the temple in Jerusalem. They expand its meaning. God's presence can fill a building—and it surely dwells within our risen Lord—but it is not confined there. God is infinite, present everywhere. When Jesus spoke with the Samaritan woman at the well, he did not abolish the temple. His words prepared his people to worship faithfully even when a building was beyond reach, "The hour is coming … when neither on this mountain nor in Jerusalem will you worship the Father … the true worshippers will worship the Father in spirit and truth" (John 4:21,23). Spirit and truth are consolations for exile—expressions of worship sustained until the House of the Lord is restored.

Whether it's an animal, produce from the field, or a heartfelt prayer, God wants worship that is pure, sincere, and offered in truth. That doesn't mean that prayer in a cathedral at sunrise is better than a lamb on the temple altar at evening. The two modes, physical and spiritual, exist together, Levitical wisdom informing the spiritual worship for all who call upon the Lord. Together, these expressions give everyone a way to draw near to God, no matter who they are or where they find themselves.

FINAL THOUGHTS

Jesus carried a deep, lonely burden for the earthly house of the Lord. He defended it, he judged it, and he wept over its impending destruction and the exile of his people into the nations. Leading worship in spirit and truth was central to his mission, but it wasn't the cause of the temple's downfall in the first century—and it doesn't explain why temple worship is absent today. These realities are tied to the covenant consequences outlined in the Mosaic covenant, a covenant that remains intact and ongoing. Because of this, Levitical worship remains a legitimate way for the people of God people to honor him, even when it cannot be fully practiced in a temple.

Right now, Jewish worship in a Jerusalem temple isn't possible. The mount itself remains one of the most contested pieces of land on earth, a place where theology and geopolitics collide. Yet God's story has never been incidental.

If the Jewish people, with support from the nations, were to resume sacrifices on or near the Temple Mount, it would be both miraculous and entirely consistent with Scripture. Many Christians would celebrate it as prophetic fulfillment, while others would likely frown upon it or even condemn it outright. But the reinstitution of temple worship is not something Christians need to oppose. It has never competed with the Messiah's sacrifice. Rather, it has always been the means by which Israel hosts God's presence among them.

In its absence, spiritual worship has always been acceptable to God. Prayer, fasting, and acts of charity are things he deeply values when offered from a humble, contrite heart. But that doesn't make spiritual worship superior to Levitical worship. The two have always existed in harmony. Both are distinct, both are pleasing, and both draw us closer to the God of life when offered in humility.

12

LEVITICUS, REIMAGINED

IF YOU'RE ANYTHING LIKE ME, this book has probably left you feeling curious, challenged, and at times, overwhelmed. I've asked you to consider in a small stack of pages what took me years to untangle. Let's pause and take stock of what we've uncovered.

THE OLD WAY OF READING LEVITICUS
Many Christians understand Leviticus through some version of these assumptions:

- Jesus abolished Leviticus by "fulfilling" its requirements in his life, making its teachings obsolete.

- The prophets pointed to a Savior whose sacrifice would replace the need for temple rituals and animal offerings.

- The first believers and the apostles abandoned their Jewish practices and created a new, "Christian" faith apart from the Torah and Judaism.

- The apostles taught salvation through faith and not through obeying the Old Testament law. At the Council of Jerusalem they even released Gentiles (and by implication believing Jews) from all law observance because of Jesus.

- Hebrews shows that Leviticus no longer matters because Jesus ended it.

- The new covenant freed believers from the law, replacing it with "grace."

- The destruction of the temple proves God is finished with Levitical worship.

From these ideas flow some common responses: many dismiss Leviticus altogether, moving past it as though it has nothing left to say. Others, especially within older traditions, honor it as sacred but transform its meaning—seeing its sacrifices and priesthood transfigured into the Church's sacramental life. Still others, especially in Evangelical circles, fear that emphasizing it might overshadow the grace revealed at the cross. Yet all of these responses, however well-intentioned, essentially spring from the same root assumption: that, in some way, Jesus replaced Leviticus.

THE TRUTHS WE'VE RECOVERED

But as we've seen, these responses lose their force when weighed against the story of Scripture and its messianic trajectory. When we let Scripture interpret itself, a different picture emerges:

- Jesus, a faithful Jew, practiced Leviticus. He upheld Torah's authority and declared it would remain the standard until heaven and earth pass away (which is also when he will have fulfilled all that the Torah and Prophets teach).

- The prophets unambiguously envision Levitical worship continuing into the future.

- The apostles and early believers, all faithful Jews, continued to practice Leviticus with conviction and joy alongside their faith in the Messiah.

- Apostolic teaching does not support the idea that Jesus replaced Leviticus with himself. The real issue in the apostolic era was Gentile inclusion and Jewish legal status—not whether Levitical rites or Torah obedience still mattered. In fact, the Council of Jerusalem imposed distinctly Levitical prohibitions on Gentiles for the sake of unity.

- Hebrews doesn't override Leviticus. It uses the temple and its patterns to explain the Messiah's work in the heavenly realm—a realm that still awaits its arrival to the land. Leviticus governs worship in this age; Messiah secures the eternal realities it anticipates for the world to come.

- The new covenant does not abolish the Torah but renews Israel's capacity for faithfulness by God's Spirit, writing Torah on their hearts.

- The absence of a temple today reflects an ongoing covenantal pattern of judgment and restoration—not a permanent end to Levitical worship.

Seen in this way, Leviticus is no relic to be transformed, nor do its practices threaten our faith in Jesus. It is the glittering centerpiece of God's enduring plan—a living anchor to the story he is still telling. Christian tradition has often spiritualized these realities, recasting itself as God's new people and dulling our imagination for how he intends to set creation right. In doing so, we've forfeited the chance to participate more fully in his plan. Leviticus still offers us a way back—a chance to bear witness to the story of Jesus in ways that Christian tradition, broken off and gone another way, has struggled to see.

Rediscovering Leviticus returns us to the place where that story was never broken. Jesus and his first followers learned to live within that story, navigating the mingling of tradition and messianic hope with grace. The question is whether we can find that grace again. Do we have the courage and humility to accept their testimony in the first place? Will we allow ourselves to see the good news they believed with fresh eyes—that God's faithfulness to Israel is the hope of the whole world?

LEARNING TO LIVE THE STORY AGAIN

Reimagining Leviticus isn't just about believing new truths—it's about learning to live as people who remember its good news. I have no desire to give my readers a checklist for faith practice or to turn Christianity into a sect of Judaism. But if these pages have done their work, perhaps they have simply awakened a sober reality—that the good news of Leviticus really has been forgotten. So what might it look like for Gentile believers today to recall Leviticus within its own story? We live far from the apostolic age and are not called to bear Israel's full covenant obligations. But still, we are invited to participate in the covenant's life.

The first place to begin is by looking humbly at Leviticus itself. Many of us have read it only in fragments, often dividing up its commands and skimming only the parts that seem relevant to us. But these methods are our own invention, not Scripture's. We may claim to honor the moral commands, but in Leviticus, every command is moral. Each one teaches how a people dwelling near the presence of God are to live. That truth still holds for us today. Leviticus invites us to return to what we've overlooked—not to reenact rituals we cannot keep, but to let their wisdom and story reshape how we worship God and how we see ourselves and our communities. Honest reflection begins where humility meets curiosity, and where obedience can once again grow from understanding.

Another natural place to begin seems to be with time itself. The first thing God called holy in Scripture was not a place or an object, but a day—the Sabbath. God never revoked or reassigned it to Sunday; he has always invited Gentiles to participate in its gift. Remembering the Sabbath reminds us of redemption we have and the greater one still to come. It points to the promise of ultimate rest. Sabbath is not about legalism or avoidance of activity; it's about grace. Where Evangelicals often say grace has freed us from Shabbat, I would say Shabbat is the living expression of grace itself. You intentionally do nothing—and God still loves you. Why would anyone want to be freed from that? Christians are quick to note that the apostles never made Sabbath a requirement for Gentiles, but perhaps that's the wrong observation. Instead of asking, "Do we have to?" and searching for ways to wriggle free of obligation, Leviticus asks, "Why wouldn't you want to?"

In our home, we welcome Shabbat with a meal on Friday night. We light candles, break the bread and pour the cup, bless the children, and enjoy the meal before us. The adults try to guide the conversation toward reflection: *"Where did you see God's goodness this week?" "Who remembers the story from the Torah we read?" "What can we work on as a family in the week to come?"* On Saturday, we try to intentionally set aside time for rest, family, and renewal. It isn't perfect, and we don't claim to be sabbath observant. We're not part of a faith community that shares this tradition, and we still worship with believers on Sunday.

But Shabbat roots us in something older than Sunday morning. Every week it reminds us what it means to stop and welcome his presence right there in our home. As I look around the table filled with family and friends, I find my heart longing more deeply for Shabbat in the Kingdom: the marriage supper of the Lamb, when rest and joy with God's family will never end.

The same is true of the biblical festivals. Passover, Shavuot, Yom Kippur, Tabernacles—these are not merely Jewish holidays but biblical ones, divine appointments when God meets with his people to rehearse the story of redemption. In honoring the festivals (imperfectly as we do), we're careful not to tread on Jewish custom, as though our participation somehow evangelizes away the Jewish nature of these sacred times. We do not claim Israel's identity for ourselves. We seek neither to Christianize the festivals nor to Judaize our faith. We simply offer our worship to God and ask him to bless the people through whom he is still keeping his promises. In faith, we stand in humble solidarity with the people to whom God has bound himself and give thanks for their Messiah, who has become our own.

Many churches have already begun taking small steps in this direction. Messianic seders help believers encounter Passover through the lens of Jesus. In a bold experiment of faith, one Lutheran congregation in our area recently set aside Sunday services throughout the year to coincide with the biblical feasts. The result was beautiful—an immersive reminder to a sanctuary full of Gentiles that God is not finished with what he began, and that even though Christians have developed their own liturgical calendar, God still keeps his.

There is, of course, room for the Christian times of Easter, Christmas, Lent, and others. But we would be wise to recognize that these holidays orbit around different themes—some of which do not rehearse God's plan for redemption as delicately and conceptually as the Levitical calendar. The goal of observing these biblical cycles isn't to become Jewish or fool ourselves into thinking we might win Jews for Christ, but to bear witness and preach to our own hearts: *This story we believe is still alive. God's covenant still stands. These people—and their destiny—still matters. Their God is our God.*

We can also return to what the psalmist calls *delight*: meditating on the Torah day and night (Psalm 1:2). The one who is blessed is not the one who delegates study to a pastor, scholar, or the safety of inherited tradition, but the one who returns to the text personally—prayerfully, and in community, again and again. Jewish meditation literature like the Torah is not about mastering information but about letting its wisdom shape the kind of people we become. It teaches us to love what God loves, to see the world as he does, and to hear his voice in the same words that formed Israel's worship and Jesus's own understanding of faithfulness. All of Scripture is worthy of our devoted study—and I spend much of my own time in every part of it—but Evangelical Christianity has terribly neglected the Torah, de-emphasizing its authority and often reading it through interpretive traditions foreign to its authors. The psalmist invites us to return to the Torah, the rich soil from which every later word of God took root.

These are small steps, and we don't have to take them all at once. There is room for a journey here—room for curiosity, growth, and learning. But recovering Leviticus starts with a renewed awareness that it's been neglected. Its wisdom still speaks, inviting us to live as though we believe it.

THE FAITH TO BELIEVE

Recovering Leviticus as good news is not merely a matter of practice. At the core, it's a matter of faith. To take it on its own terms means letting this forgotten story reshape how we think about God, his covenant, and ourselves. It challenges the gospel we've grown comfortable with—the one centered on us, our salvation, traditions, and motives. If Leviticus truly matters as Scripture presents it, then much of what we believe about Jesus, the Bible, and God's plan for the world must be reexamined.

The real challenge is not only theological—it is eschatological. What we believe about the end shapes how we live now. When we treat

Leviticus as something Jesus replaced, we preserve a Christian-centric gospel detached from the people and promises that first gave it meaning. In that reading Leviticus becomes a relic, salvation becomes the pinnacle, the cross our finish line, Jesus our savior. The gospel, stripped of Abraham's promises, becomes an eternity emptied of Leviticus and every reality it reflects. But Jesus and the biblical authors knew the secret of Leviticus: it is a blueprint for the age to come, a testimony to God's intent to dwell with Israel and bless the nations through them.

Abraham understood that secret. He believed God's promise long before the Torah, temple, priesthood, or even a Messiah. His faith was not in a system or in Jesus, but in the God who keeps his word. Abraham believed in the gospel first spoken through the Torah—that through his family all nations would be blessed. God counted Abraham righteous because of it. That same faith is what remembering Leviticus demands of us. It asks us to believe that God's covenant with Israel still stands, even in the face of all the odds and interpretations we have stacked against it. Leviticus demands we believe that his promises have not failed or been rewritten, and that his presence will again be among his people—that the root of Jesse has sprung forth to accomplish it and will see it all the way through.

Paul warned Gentile believers not to boast against that root. Though graciously grafted in, we are not the natural plant (Romans 11). But Christian tradition has often lived as though the root no longer matters—spiritualizing the covenant, claiming the blessings, recasting Jesus apart from his Jewish calling, and forgetting the people through whom those blessings come. But we do not have to remain that way.

To Gentile believers, God extends an extraordinary invitation: to participate in bringing his promises to fulfillment—for Israel and through Israel. Our faith in Israel's Messiah, and in the story that formed him, declares to the world that God will do what he said. When we trust in the promises God made to Israel—with the same faith Abraham showed—we become catalysts in Israel's own awakening. In declaring this hope, we speak not only to the Jewish people, but to ourselves and to a watching world: the God who came down at Sinai—who wed himself to a people and revealed his heart in fire and smoke—is faithful. He will come through again. Our steadfast hope reminds Israel that their God has not abandoned them. Our testimony stirs a holy jealousy for what is rightfully theirs, and our confidence in their story draws their hearts back toward the door of the fallen tent that has stood silent for so long in their midst (Romans 11:11).

We worship a God who raises the dead. Abraham believed he could raise Isaac. We believe he raised Jesus and has raised us from death in sin. But it takes faith greater still—faith like Abraham's—to believe he will raise Israel. Leviticus calls us to proclaim a gospel that is costly, disruptive, and deeper than the one we often settle for. It does not merely ask us to trust in God's faithfulness to us; it asks us to trust his faithfulness to them.

And that is the heart of Leviticus. It is not a relic of ancient law, but the evidence of a promise we still await: God bringing his glorious presence here, among humanity in this land, once again. Leviticus is the heartbeat of that story—a story that humbles Christian pride, moves us out of the center, and restores us to the covenant we were always meant to share with the people to whom it belongs. When we stop rewriting God's promises and believe that God will do exactly what he said, the Prophets' final line bursts to life: "And He will turn the hearts of fathers to their children, and the hearts of children to their fathers" (Malachi 4:6).

The fallen tent, the reassigned promises, the reinterpreted rituals, the overlooked people—these can become bridges back to the God of Abraham. Leviticus is not merely the shadow of what God once did for us in Jesus; it is the enduring testimony of what he still intends to do—for Israel, for us, and for all the world. Our faith in that long lost good news invites us to join the cry for the coming of the Lord, together with the people who have been expecting him for so very long.

WHEN LEVITICUS COMES TRUE

For Christians, the greatest hope of our faith is that Leviticus comes true. All we hope for is a future when we will live forever, perfected, whole, and at rest in the abundant life and love of Yahweh. That hope depends on Israel's awakening to her Messiah—when, in God's time and by his way, her restoration will renew all creation (Romans 11:15). But our greatest hope is also our heaviest task. To participate in the restoration of the covenant family, we must first submit to the circumcision of our own hearts. Faith like Abraham's requires us to cut through the most vulnerable parts of ourselves—our rank, our reputations, our long-held traditions and assumptions. We place them on the altar in surrender. In doing so, we become living sacrifices ourselves.

Leviticus teaches us to lay down what we hold most dear and approach the divine tent in humility through the representatives he appointed to guard his presence and keep his covenant. For too long, Christianity has waltzed past those keepers, flashing our "Jesus card" like a backstage pass. *We have Jesus. Let us through.* Like Korah, we rebel: *Who do you think you are? There is no distinction between us. We're just as holy.* Like Cain, we rage at God's favor toward our brother: *What you have to offer is no better. There's no more need for you.* And so, we echo the words of Israel's enemies: *You are an outcast. You are forgotten. You mean nothing.*

But there is another path, narrow but well-worn by the faithful who walked it before us. We can be like Jonathan, who laid down his claim to the throne and pledged allegiance to God's anointed one through a covenant. We can be like Ruth, who joined herself to Naomi and to Israel's God—not for her own benefit, but to see the restoration of all that Naomi had lost. We can be like Cornelius, who worshipped God faithfully from far outside the camp, but never wavered in believing that God would one day restore those inside.

Leviticus beckons us to study the ancient ways and recover a message that blesses the very people upon whom God's promises rest. As we fix our eyes on the things above, we help turn Israel's gaze to the door of the tent. They listen for his voice, for the footsteps of the one who brings good news. They wait—longing, with all who call upon the Lord—for the day that their Anointed One emerges from the most holy place, opening a fountain to purify them forever.

That day is our hope.

Vayikra. And He Calls is still calling.

May we have ears to hear the forgotten gospel—the good news still echoing through the tent of the one who speaks.

APPENDIX

ON COVENANT, CONTINUITY, AND THE STORY OF LEVITICUS

INTRODUCTION

Scripture tells a covenantal story—a single, living relationship through which God binds himself to his people. Each covenant deepens that relationship, expanding its promises without erasing what came before. From Adam to Abraham, from Sinai to David, from the prophets to the Messiah, the story of the Bible is the story of God's unwavering commitment to dwell among his creation and fulfill his promises. None of these covenants are temporary contracts or evolving modes of grace. They are layers of the same unbreakable promise.

This section is written for readers who want to go deeper and for those who wish to see how the ideas explored in this book fit within the broader landscape of Christian theology. It traces how covenant continuity has been understood throughout church history, exploring the major systems that sought to explain the relationship between Israel and the church. It also considers how Catholic, Orthodox, and Protestant traditions have framed the law, and how more recent recovery movements have tried to return to Scripture's Jewish roots.

My aim here is not only to critique those frameworks but to draw out what they reveal about our shared longing for understanding—for a God whose faithfulness holds our shared hope together. By surveying these theological approaches and setting them alongside the integrated vision of covenant found in the Torah (especially in Leviticus) this section argues that God's covenant faithfulness has never shifted from Israel but continues onward through her calling and Messiah to embrace the nations and bring God's purposes to their intended goal.

PART I: THE WHOLE COVENANT–A UNIFIED VIEW OF GOD'S PROMISE

I approach Scripture from a holistic, unified standpoint. That means I see Scripture's covenants as integrated, expansive, and centered on one people—Israel, led by the Messiah. This is not how most theological systems approach them.

Supersessionism, Covenant Theology, Dispensationalism, and Progressive Covenant views are all, in essence, Replacement Theology. In their own ways, each divests the land of Israel and the Jewish people from the promises of God. They separate the covenant from the people and promises of the story, and in doing so, they strip the covenant of its relational fabric.

Each system, though different in form, redefines covenant as a mechanism of theology rather than the heartbeat of God's ongoing commitment to Israel and the nations, reshaping it to accommodate the church in ways the biblical story itself does not. In the process, Leviticus—and the entire tradition of worship it represents—is relegated to a past era, no longer vital to the covenant story.

But it is my conviction that Leviticus is not a relic; it is the means by which the covenant gift of Sinai—God's dwelling among his people—is made possible. To consign it to history, parcel it into parts, or to transcend its functions through Mass, sacrament, or other Christian forms of worship, empties God's promise of its substance and intended purpose. God did not covenant to dwell among Christians; he covenanted to dwell with *Israel.* The Messiah's priesthood does not abolish that covenantal logic but perfects it—securing Leviticus's promise of nearness on an eschatological level for all who align with Israel's king. When Jesus spoke of a day coming when people would worship "in spirit and in truth," he was not canceling Sinai's greatest gift but extending grace within its absence—a consolation for exile, not a replacement for presence.

PART II: HOW THEOLOGY FRAMES COVENANT

Across history, the church has developed a variety of theological systems to explain how God's covenants fit together. Each framework arose from a genuine desire to honor Scripture and safeguard the gospel. What follows is a brief survey of these major theologies—how they framed covenant continuity, where they preserved truth (or parts of it), and where I believe they diverge from the covenant's original scope and intent.

Supersessionism—The Erasure of Israel

These related views hold that the Church has replaced Israel as God's covenant people. Classic supersessionism holds that Israel is fully nullified and replaced; softer views hold that Israel's role is absorbed into the Church, and a practical supersessionism assumes replacement through habits and teaching, rather than an outright rejection of Israel. In these views, God's promises to Israel remain true, but only in a symbolic or "fulfilled" sense, or in the sense that those promises were always meant for the true Israel—understood to be the Christian Church. Historically, this view developed as Christianity sought to define itself apart from Judaism, especially after the destruction of the Second Temple and the spread of the church in the Roman world. Some versions of supersessionism are explicit, teaching that Israel's role in salvation history has ended; others are more implicit, assuming that Old Testament promises find their complete realization in Christ and therefore no longer apply to ethnic or national Israel. In both cases, the result is the same: Israel's continuing covenant role in God's redemptive plan is minimized or erased. Supersessionism is ***replacement through erasure***—Israel's covenant identity is effectively written out of the story.

> **Where I Overlap:** I stand almost entirely against this view, except for one nuanced area—though it's more linguistic than theological. I agree that the covenants find their full meaning in Messiah, but that meaning does not annul or spiritualize them. It also has not yet happened in full.

Where I Diverge: This view fails to take seriously the ongoing election of Israel and the permanence of God's promises. Scripture never portrays the Church as replacing Israel, but as being grafted into her story (Romans 11). Paul's olive-tree metaphor captures this perfectly: continuity, not succession; inclusion with distinction, not displacement. I see tremendous danger in the alternative. When Christians become the "true Israel," what does that make the Jewish people? No people at all? Once a people are erased in theory, it is only a matter of time before someone tries to erase them in fact. The belief that Christianity was the "true Israel"—common among many early church leaders—produced some of the worst expressions of hatred and violence toward the Jewish people in history.

Covenant Theology—The Unity That Over-Spiritualized
Rooted in the Reformed tradition, Covenant Theology frames all of God's dealings with humanity through two or three overarching theological covenants (works, grace, and redemption). This system preserves a sense of unity within Scripture but often does so by spiritualizing the biblical covenants themselves—treating them as theological categories in salvation history rather than as relational commitments with a specific people. It also essentially treats Israel and the church as one and the same. The promises to Abraham are understood to belong to the church and Christians, rather than to a particular nation. The result is that ethnic Israel's ongoing role in God's purposes is often subsumed under the universal church, with "Israel" redefined as a purely spiritual community composed of all who believe in Christ. Covenant Theology is ***replacement through spiritualization***—Israel's promises are reinterpreted as universal, belonging to the church rather than to a distinct people.

Where I Overlap: I share the conviction that God's purposes are unified from Genesis to Revelation.

Where I Diverge: God's promises to Abraham, Israel, and David remain active and distinct because his faithfulness is not theoretical. It is bound to the people with whom he made those covenants. To detach those promises from Israel turns the work of Jesus into metaphor, robs the Jewish people of God's enduring promises, and reduces divine faithfulness to a mere concept rather than a lived—and much hoped for—reality.

Dispensationalism—Two Stories, Not One

Dispensational theology, popularized in the nineteenth and twentieth centuries, divides history into separate "dispensations" or eras in which God relates to humanity, dispensing his grace in different ways. It famously preserves a future hope for Israel but separates the church into a distinct program of redemption, often called the Church Age. During this age, God is at work in the world, revealing himself through Christians and the church, not through Israel. It is the main mode of interpretation within American Evangelicalism. Dispensationalism's strength lies in its high regard for the plain meaning of Scripture and its insistence that God will remain faithful to his promises to Israel. But by rigidly dividing God's redemptive work between Israel and the church, it fragments the unity of the biblical story, minimizes the calling of Israel, and deemphasizes the oneness of Jew and Gentile in Messiah. Dispensationalism is ***replacement through division***—Israel and the church are separated into different redemptive programs, with Israel's role temporarily set aside.

Where I Overlap: I agree that God's promises to Israel endure and that his covenant with them is not nullified. Israel remains central to God's redemptive purposes.

Where I Diverge: Dispensationalism fractures the unity of Scripture and tells two parallel stories of redemption—one for Israel and one for the church. The Bible tells one story of a covenant-keeping God who invites the nations into Israel's promises. God does not suspend his covenantal commitment to Israel in order to work temporarily through another people, only to return to Israel later. His purpose for Israel remains continuous and operative, and the nations have always been included within that single, unfolding plan.

Progressive Covenant and Inclusion Theology—
Expanding the Circle, Erasing the Lines

A more recent development, this family of views teaches that Jesus inaugurated a *new* covenant that fulfills and thereby renders all previous covenants—including the Mosaic—no longer binding in their original form. It avoids the pitfalls of a rigid dispensationalism and an overly spiritual covenant theology. The moral vision of the Torah is said to continue through Christ and the Spirit, but its ritual, priestly, national, and geographic dimensions are regarded as having reached their end or transformation in him. The Old Testament's promises function as typological foreshadows of greater realities fulfilled in Christ. The temple, as one example, represents God's dwelling with humanity, now made complete in Jesus and through the Spirit's presence. Israel collapses into Messiah, and there is a redefinition of the people of God. Inclusion Theology extends this logic, emphasizing that all people are now equally included in the new covenant through faith in Christ, without distinction between Jew and Gentile, and that the everyone with faith in Christ has inherited the promises once given to Israel. Progressive Covenant Theology is **replacement through absorption**—Israel and the church are blended into a single, indistinguishable entity, dissolving their covenantal distinctives.

> **Where I Overlap:** I agree that Jesus's death cut the new covenant, that he fulfills the covenant story and embodies its intent, that Gentiles will participate in the covenant's blessings, and that there is hope for Israel in Messiah.

Where I Diverge: The "new covenant" of Jeremiah 31 is explicitly made with the house of Israel and the house of Judah. The Messiah's blood ratifies the promise for Israel first, and through him, that mercy overflows to the nations. Where progressive systems describe continuity as transformation, I describe it as endurance—the same covenant continuing in new conditions, not a reconstitution of its terms. In this covenant, Jew and Gentile remain distinct, yet united in worship under the same Messiah. The fulfillment of this covenant is still in progress—tied to the endurance of heaven and earth and awaiting its completion during the Messiah's reign from Jerusalem.

The Jewish Vision: The Covenant Renewed and Strengthened
Although not a traditional Christian view, because God's covenant was made with Israel—and not with the church—I believe it is vital to consider how the Jewish tradition understands it. It is, after all, *their* covenant, recorded and preserved by their prophets and scribes, so their interpretation, in my view, carries significant weight.

Within Jewish tradition, Jeremiah's "new covenant" has never been read as a replacement for Sinai's, but as its renewal. The Hebrew word *chadash* can mean "new" or "renewed," and rabbinic commentators have consistently understood the passage to describe a future moment when Israel's obedience will be perfected, not when the Torah will be abolished. The same covenant—written on the heart instead of stone— remains the foundation. In this view, the "new covenant" is not a new law, a new people, or even to some extent a new covenant, but a new capacity for faithfulness.

This vision anticipates a time when Israel, fully restored and indwelt by the Spirit of God, will embody the Torah's wisdom as naturally as breathing. This Torah will flow like a river, bringing life and blessing to the nations, who will be eager to learn it. It is eschatological, not super- seding; it looks forward to the same covenant fulfilled, not a different one introduced. The Jewish hope of Jeremiah 31 and the Christian hope of eternal life share the same longing—the restoration of God's presence and the renewal of all things—but they come by that hope through different mechanisms. **The Jewish view is *renewal, not replacement*—**the new covenant reaffirms Sinai's covenant, promising a future restoration of Israel's obedience (and its subsequent fulfillment of God's blessings to the nations) rather than a new law or people.

> **Where I Overlap:** I share the conviction that Jeremiah's covenant is a renewal, not a replacement. Like the Jewish view, I see the Torah as enduring and the new covenant as the internalization of that same covenant faithfulness. I also agree that this promise is made first and foremost to Israel, and that Israel's full recognition of the Messiah will bring about the age of restoration and the divine presence.

> **Where I Diverge:** I believe that this renewal has already (partially) begun through Israel's Messiah, Jesus, whose blood cut the new covenant and inaugurated its promises. While the Jewish reading (and my own) awaits Israel's national redemption, Scripture, the testimony of Jesus, and the witness of the Spirit all reveal that this renewal has already broken into history—though its full completion still awaits the day when all Israel is redeemed. In that sense, I hold that the covenant remains Jewish in origin, scope, and fulfillment, yet its blessings have already begun to bring a foretaste of renewal: first among the enduring and distinct Jewish remnant, and subsequently, in the nations, through faith in Israel's Messiah—without diminishing Israel's primacy or distinctive, ongoing identity in that story.

PART III: HOW TRADITIONS FRAME COVENANTS

Over the centuries, each branch of the church has sought to explain how the covenants of Scripture reach their fulfillment in Christ and how Israel's story continues—or doesn't—within that framework. These interpretations were born from sincere theological reflection and historical necessity, yet each tradition reshaped Leviticus and the Torah in distinct ways. What follows explores how Catholic, Orthodox, and

Protestant traditions each sought to preserve the unity of Scripture—and how, in doing so, they sometimes blurred the covenant's living connection to Israel.

Catholic Theology: Fulfillment by Elevation

Catholic theology has long resisted the charge of supersessionism, at least in its official teaching. The Church does not claim that God's covenant with Israel was revoked or that his promises have failed. In fact, the *Catechism* explicitly affirms that the old covenant has never been revoked (CCC 121–23) and that Israel remains permanently bound to God's purposes (CCC 839–40). In this sense, Catholic theology maintains a continuity that much of Protestantism has lost: it holds that the covenants are successive stages in one divine plan, not a series of abandoned experiments.

Yet even with this affirmation, the practical outcome still resembles a kind of soft supersessionism. Within Catholic thought, the covenant with Israel is said to reach its perfection and transfiguration in Christ and the Church. The sacrificial system, priesthood, and sanctuary of Leviticus are understood as having been fulfilled and elevated into a higher reality—the Eucharistic sacrifice of the Mass. The logic is not replacement by rejection, but replacement by elevation: the old is redefined by the new, its meaning carried forward but its practice surpassed.

In that sense, Catholic theology preserves Leviticus symbolically but not substantively. The Law is honored as revelation (and Israel is still acknowledged, at least in principle, as having an enduring role in God's plan), yet in practice that role is absorbed into the Church's own life. Its ritual, priestly, and calendrical dimensions find their true and final expression in the Church's sacramental worship.

My view differs here. I agree that Leviticus finds its deepest meaning in the Messiah, but not because its forms have been transcended or elevated. Rather, its original meaning continues—alive, instructive, prophetic, and eschatological—still teaching the people of God how nearness to him is bound together with the people he covenanted with: the Jews.

Orthodox Theology: Transfiguration of the Law

The Orthodox Church, like the Catholic tradition, has never rejected the Torah outright but reads it through the lens of divine mystery. In Eastern theology, the law serves as a preparation for *theosis*—the transformation of humanity through participation in God's life. Levitical worship is not discarded but transfigured; its sacrifices and priesthood are seen as earthly icons of the heavenly liturgy now revealed in the Divine Liturgy. This view preserves reverence for Leviticus as sacred pattern but still lifts it out of Israel's story, relocating its meaning entirely within the Church's worship, and removed from Israel itself. Once again, the logic is replacement by elevation and transformation.

My approach differs in that I see Leviticus not only as a shadow of heavenly realities, but as a continuing and enduring system for hosting God's presence on the land—even if that reality is not currently expressed on the land. The hosting of God's presence remains the central gift of the Sinai covenant, still in effect.

Protestant Theology: Abolished for the Sake of Grace

If Catholic theology tends to subsume Leviticus through elevation—transfiguring its forms into sacraments—Protestant theology tends to set it aside through division. Seeking to safeguard the gospel of grace from any hint of legalism, the Reformers separated the Torah into distinct categories: moral, civil, and ceremonial. The moral law, they argued, remained binding as a reflection of God's righteousness, while the civil and ceremonial laws (those concerning sacrifice, purity, and priesthood) were fulfilled and thus abolished in Christ.

Anglican theology, the "middle way" between Catholic and Reformed traditions, retained this division while preserving a more liturgical continuity with Rome. In practice, it too treats Leviticus as symbolically fulfilled in Christ rather than as an active source of instruction. Even where Protestant theology affirms continuity with the Old Testament, it often confines that continuity to ethics. The Law survives as moral principle, but not as covenantal reality. As a result, Leviticus is read symbolically, moralized, or mined for metaphors about sin and holiness—honored for its historical value, yet rarely celebrated as a living witness to God's ongoing promises to Israel and the nations.

My perspective moves in another direction. I affirm with the Reformers that salvation comes by grace through faith in the work of the Messiah, yet I hold that the Torah and God's covenant promises form the foundation of that faith. In my view, faith in the Messiah cannot be fully understood apart from the story that defines him; it only finds coherence within the covenant framework that reveals who he is and what God intends him to do. Leviticus, then, is not law opposed to gospel, but instructions within the story of the gospel. It unveils grace in its original form: a holy God coming close to his people and teaching them how to dwell with him.

PART IV: THE TRADITIONAL THREEFOLD DIVISION OF LAW AND ITS LIMITS

Since the Reformation, most Protestant theologians have explained the Torah through a threefold distinction: moral, civil, and ceremonial law. By contrast, Catholic theology has typically understood the Mosaic law as finding its fulfillment and elevation in Christ through the sacraments and canon law, rather than by dividing it into parts; Eastern Orthodox theology has never formally adopted such a threefold scheme, viewing the law more as a mystical foreshadowing of divine life in Christ than a legal system to be parsed. Regardless of tradition, many Christians land somewhere in the middle and often acknowledge some division of the law in some form.

The Protestant framework—first articulated by Thomas Aquinas and later modified by John Calvin—was meant to preserve continuity between the Old and New Testaments while explaining why Protestants no longer follow Israel's ritual or civic laws. The moral law, they argued, reveals God's unchanging character and remains binding; the civil and ceremonial laws applied only to ancient Israel and were fulfilled by Christ. This model served a purpose in its time. It allowed the Reformers to retain the Old Testament as Scripture while distinguishing themselves from both Judaism and the medieval sacramental system they sought to reform.

Yet the framework itself is foreign to the Torah. Leviticus presents the laws as an integrated fabric shaping the kind of people among whom God's presence dwells. To divide or dismiss them disrupts the wisdom these commands provide to guide his people through time and across circumstances.

Leviticus and the Indivisible Story of Holiness

Leviticus shows no hierarchy between moral and ritual life. The same God who commands honesty in business (a moral/civil category; 19:35–36) commands purity in worship (ritual; 11–15), justice in judgment (civil; 19:15), and reverence for the Sabbath (ritual; 23:3). These are not separate categories but one unified way of life of a community ordered around God's presence. Dividing them turns holiness into an abstraction—something we can affirm in theory while neglecting in practice.

Modern Christianity, especially within Evangelicalism, has often excelled at this abstraction. It's easy to claim that understanding the *intent* of the law is enough—as though insight replaces, or at least blurs, obedience—"making it a matter of the heart" in many instances. This has produced an attitude that knowing the intent of the law excuses one from practicing it. In extending Jesus's seemingly flexible interpretations of Torah beyond their context, many Christians have, in effect, dismissed the Torah altogether. The result is inconsistency.

Marriage offers a prime example. Across Christian traditions, the standard for what constitutes marriage—and who may marry—varies widely, sometimes straying far from the Torah's wisdom. (To be fair, certain branches of Judaism have also wandered from Torah's vision in this area.) In the Torah, the boundaries surrounding marriage and sexual ethics are moral concerns, not solely ceremonial ones, because they safeguard holiness in the most intimate parts of human life. While Christianity often affirms that the moral commands of the Torah still stand, it frequently disagrees with the Torah about what those moral standards actually are.

A related area that reveals the same problem involves laws about reproductive fluids and menstruation. These are often dismissed in Christianity as obsolete purity laws tied to the temple, yet some of them are moral prohibitions that apply outside the sanctuary. For example, the Torah forbids sexual relations during menstruation—not only as a matter of ritual impurity, but as a matter of holiness and respect for the keeping the marriage bed undefiled. The apostles upheld this same ethic when they prohibited "sexual immorality" in Acts 15 and Hebrews 13:4, a term that assumes the Torah's specific definitions. But within Christianity, this connection is rarely acknowledged and almost never discussed. It's another way Christianity often claims to uphold the moral law while quietly redefining, or simply ignoring, its boundaries.

This inconsistency is not limited to questions of sexual ethics; it extends into ceremonial matters as well, with the Sabbath serving as a prime example. Christian tradition affirms the Ten Commandments, and "remembering the Sabbath" is one of them. Yet the Sabbath in view is not Sunday, but the period from Friday sundown to Saturday sundown. Within Christianity, this command has been interpreted in widely varying ways, despite the fact that it clearly falls within what modern theology would classify as a ceremonial or calendrical law. For some, Sabbath observance entails a full cessation from activity; for others, it means refraining only from ordinary labor performed on the other six days. Still others regard it as simply maintaining a mental awareness that the day is special. In contemporary practice, it may even mean taking any day off during the week, regardless of whether it coincides with the biblical Sabbath. Among many within relaxed Evangelical contexts, the concept has been reduced further—often to an hour of church attendance (and sometimes only on weeks when it is convenient).

The flaw lies not in the division of the law itself or even diversity of practice, but in the attempt to define the morality of the Torah according to human intuition and traditional preference. Leviticus, by contrast, does not partition holiness into categories of observance or exemption. It does not leave holiness to interpretation; it defines it, and expects those who would dwell with God to embody it.

Jesus reinforces this. He rebukes those who tithe while neglecting justice and mercy (Matthew 23:23)—not because pure morality replaced the ritual of tithing, but because the Torah's integrated vision of holiness was being fractured. Likewise, Paul's engagement with the law is not a rejection or redefinition of its ritual or civil dimensions, but a defense of covenant access for Gentiles without conversion. His concern is not with the "categories" law itself, but with its misuse to exclude those whom God was welcoming in.

For clarity, it should be noted that Leviticus—and indeed the entire Torah—does make distinctions. Some commands apply only to particular groups (priests, men, women of childbearing age, Nazirites, etc.) and some commands are dependent on the sanctuary's presence and one's proximity to it. Yet there are also clear examples of laws that Christians later labeled civic, moral, and ritual being applied equally to Gentiles living among ancient Israel. Sojourners were expected to rest on the Sabbath (sundown Friday to sundown Saturday, Exodus 20:10), abstain from eating blood (Leviticus 17:10–13), participate in the Day of Atonement fast (Leviticus 16:29), and uphold the same standards of justice and honesty as the native-born (Leviticus 24:22; Numbers 15:15–16). The Torah's concern is not only ethnic boundary or legal category but communal holiness—a unified story teaching every generation how to dwell with God.

The apostles carried this same Torah logic into their own context, applying to Gentile believers the same commands the Torah gave to sojourners: practices that preserved unity and holiness among those joined to Israel's God. This allowed Gentile disciples to retain their ethnic identity, share table fellowship with Torah-observant Jews, and still host God's presence through the Spirit within purified hearts and holy lifestyles among God's people—until the day when his presence would fill the world in full.

For Leviticus, holiness is not compartmentalized, though it is carefully organized and defined. It weaves through every dimension of

Israel's life and extends even to the outsiders who dwell among them. Where Christian tradition has often treated the law as a legal code to be divided and analyzed, the Torah reminds us that Leviticus is not the law itself. It is part of a larger story—a story in which many laws reveal the wisdom of God and shape a community meant to become the place where he dwells.

The traditional division of the law may have helped Christian theology make sense of its own history—and its self-imposed need to distinguish itself from Judaism—but in doing so, it obscured the Torah's own vision. Holiness was never meant to be sliced into moral, civil, and ceremonial parts or discarded whenever it feels foreign or irrelevant to our culture. It is one reality, one story, given to every generation as a source of wisdom for faithful, obedient living, teaching God's people how to walk in his presence and find life through Messiah (2 Timothy 3:15–16).

PART V: RECOVERY MOVEMENTS–ATTEMPTS TO RETURN TO THE ROOT

In recent decades, new developments have arisen within the Jesus movement seeking to recover the Jewish roots of faith and the ongoing relevance of the Torah. Though diverse in practice, they share a desire to return to Scripture's original context and to rejoin the story of Israel that hosts the gospel. This section considers two such movements— Hebrew Roots and Messianic Judaism—each offering a different vision for how followers of Jesus might recover Israel's faith without repeating the mistakes of the past.

Hebrew Roots and the Return to Torah

Over the last several decades, a growing number of believers have sought to recover the Jewish context of Scripture and return to the commandments of the Torah. This movement, often called Hebrew Roots or Torah Observant Christianity, challenges many traditional Christian assumptions. Its adherents emphasize Sabbath observance, the biblical feasts, and dietary laws as enduring expressions of faithfulness, and in doing so, they have helped many rediscover the richness of Scripture's Hebrew foundations.

While I share much of the desire to recover the fullness of God's story and to reflect faith in the God of Israel, I take a different path. Hebrew Roots teaching often assumes that faithfulness requires full (or mostly full) adherence to Torah law as a binding commandment for all believers. My approach is not to prescribe renewed legal observance, but to recover the redemptive meaning behind those practices. The aim in this work is not to re-establish Jewish temple ritual or impose law on Gentiles, but to re-learn what Leviticus reveals about God's redemptive plans and the story of Jesus.

The Hebrew Roots movement rightly reminds the church that God never divorced himself from Israel, but when law becomes the measure of belonging, we move backwards; the multiethnic family of God loses its diversity, and both Jew and Gentile lose their distinctive callings within his plan. The gospel of Leviticus invites Gentiles to draw near to God through the people who keep his covenant. We are not called to become Jews or bear the full yoke of Torah, but to enter the promises through the Messiah's blood and walk the path God opened among his people as we bear witness to those promises.

Messianic Judaism and the Faithfulness of God
Messianic Judaism begins with the question of identity—what it means to be Jewish and follow the Messiah of Israel. Its central concern is not so much how salvation works, but who the people of God are and how Jews and Gentiles share life together within the same covenant promises.

Messianic Jewish theology holds that God's covenants with Israel remain active, that Jewish identity is not erased in Messiah, and that the promises given through the Torah, the Prophets, and the Writings still define Israel's calling today. It insists that Jewish believers in Yeshua remain Jews—and that Gentile believers are invited to join Israel's story, not replace it. This framework profoundly shaped the perspective of this book. My approach shares its same core conviction.

Where my approach differs from Messianic Judaism is in scope, audience, and to some extent, in application. This book is written primarily for Gentile followers of Jesus within the American, Evangelical world—those who have inherited a faith largely severed from its Jewish roots. I draw from the messianic hermeneutic because I believe it interprets Scripture as Jesus and the biblical authors did: through the unity of Israel's story, the continuity of God's covenants, and the faithfulness of a Messiah who gathers both Israel and the nations into one redeemed, but diverse, people.

My purpose is unique in that I do not to teach Jewish believers how to remain faithful to the covenant. I am not in a position to do so; that's a matter for their own leadership to decide. Instead, I apply the messianic hermeneutic to awaken Gentile believers to a story they have forgotten and to the high cost of leaving it out of the gospel we proclaim.

When Gentiles neglect the ongoing covenant story of Israel, they not only fail to honor the people through whom God still keeps his promises, but they also lose sight of their own prophetic role in God's redemptive plan—announcing a gospel that has become detached from the story it arises from. Paul envisioned Gentiles so gripped by faith in Israel's promises—including the promise of God's dwelling among his people—that their faith would stir Israel to jealousy and renewed longing for those same promises.

That is the awakening my work seeks: a recovery of the gospel of the Torah—the same good news Jesus and the apostles preached—in which the nations find their hope not apart from Israel, but through her vindication and restoration under her rightful king.

PART VI: THE COVENANT STORY AS ONE THREAD

The Christian frameworks described here each attempt to explain how the Old and New Testaments fit together. All recognize continuity in some form, yet each—at least in part—severs God's holy covenant from the people with whom it was made. They imagine that God's promises can transcend the erasure, spiritualization, absorption, temporary suspension, or total definition of the very nation to whom they were given.

It is my conviction that Scripture never speaks this way. Every covenant is bound to God's commitment to the family of Abraham, to the promises he made to them, his dwelling among them, to the king installed through David's line, and to his steadfast faithfulness throughout their generations. The nations—and Christians—are not, have never been, and never will be the primary recipients of these promises. This reality neither excludes Christians from God's abundant blessings, nor alters the fact that God has bound the restoration of creation to Israel through a covenant mediated by her Messiah, Jesus of Nazareth.

The covenants are not stairs ascending to something higher, nor hallways diverging to somewhere else, nor loading docks transferring God's promised cargo to a different recipient. They are the eternal vows of a relationship God refuses to let fail.

It is the same God, the same promises, and the same people— revealed in fullness through the Messiah of Israel promised by the Hebrew Scriptures and witnessed by the writings of the New Testament. The fact that the Jewish people have not yet corporately recognized this does not make the covenant any less valid, nor does it make it any more Christian. It simply makes it part of the continuing story of Scripture.

That continuity is the heartbeat of Leviticus. To reimagine Leviticus within the ongoing, holy covenant recovers the gospel it tells: when God dwells among Israel, it is very good news.

A FINAL WORD TO MY READERS

THANK YOU FOR READING *THE FORGOTTEN GOSPEL*. It is my deep hope that this book has stretched your mind, widened your spiritual imagination, offered new ideas to ponder, and ultimately deepened your faith.

Independent publishing is a gift. It allows writers like me to share long-form work without institutional backing—and it's only possible because of the generosity of engaged readers like you. Everything I write, I make available for free. I believe cost should never be an obstacle to biblical literacy.

If this book has been helpful to you, here are a few impactful ways you can support my work:

Leave a review

Please leave a brief review of *The Forgotten Gospel* on Amazon. This is one of the most effective ways to help the book reach readers who are searching for thoughtful, faithful engagement with Scripture. You might also consider recommending this book to others through word of mouth or on social media, or even gift a copy or two to a friend. These personal recommendations remain the most meaningful way this message finds new hands.

Stay connected
You can follow me on Instagram or Facebook (@BriannaTittelAuthor), or subscribe to my blog at **briannatittel.com**. I regularly share essays, project updates, and book extras through my website and newsletter, and I invite you to read along.

Support my work financially
If you feel led to help sustain future writing and teaching projects, you can find ways to do so at my website.

MANY BLESSINGS TO YOU, AND THANK YOU FOR READING.

ACKNOWLEDGMENTS

WRITING A BOOK is at once a solitary endeavor and a team effort. I cannot share these words with the world without thanking some incredible people.

To my loving husband, Mike—my undaunted support. You believed I had a book in me long before I ever did, and you never stopped reminding me it was possible. Thank you for your unwavering conviction that this project was worth seeing through, for carrying the weight in countless unseen ways, and for championing me every step of the way.

To my parents, Ray and Carolyn, who have prayed over my life and learning since the moment I opened my eyes. Your love and generosity have sustained me in every area of life, and your contribution to this book is truly immeasurable.

To my children, who have shown such patience while I spent long hours lost in writing. Thank you for enduring the many lackluster dinners on days when I lost track of time typing away, and for celebrating all the little wins. You are my pride and joy.

To our small group, for faithfully showing up to study the hard parts of Scripture with me. The very idea for this book was born from your commitment to wrestle with Leviticus together. Without you, the questions that drive these pages might never have made it beyond the walls of my own mind!

To my editor, Paul, for taking a shot on a total unknown. Your careful eyes on the manuscript brought every line to its truest meaning and gave me the confidence to publish well.

To Tim Mackie, your teaching and example have shaped me profoundly. You encouraged my pursuit as a student of Scripture when many did not, and you showed me how to teach the Bible when I wasn't sure I could. Without your influence, I simply could not have written this book.

To all the unseen givers whose generosity made my learning possible—through words, classes, and resources shared freely, you have sown into my growth more than you will ever know.

Finally, I bow in humble gratitude at the feet of the Lord. My deepest thanks belong to him, who has been faithful to bring me along. He supplies the words, and I remain eternally humbled to be entrusted with something far greater than myself.

ENDNOTES

1   "The Digital Pulpit: A Nationwide Analysis of Online Sermons," Pew Research Center, December 19, 2019, https://www.pewresearch.org/religion/2019/12/16/the-digital-pulpit-a-nationwide-analysis-of-online-sermons/.

2   See Robert Kinney, "Leviticus and Liturgy," *Center for Pastor Theologians—Made Like Him: Reflections on Formation and Gathered Worship*," March 2, 2021, https://www.pastortheologians.com/articles/2021/3/2/leviticus-and-liturgy.

3   See Douglas J. Moo, ed., *Five Views on Law and Gospel* (Zondervan, 1996).

4   Scot McKnight, *The King Jesus Gospel* (Zondervan, 2011).

5   L. Michael Morales, *Who Shall Ascend the Mountain of the Lord* (Apollos, 2015), 23.

6   Ibid., 27.

7   I borrowed this language and adapted it for my own use from BibleProject. BibleProject is a non-profit that exists to help people understand the Bible as a unified story that leads to Jesus. I highly recommend their resources. See bibleproject.com.

8   Encyclopaedia Britannica, s.v. "Messiah," last updated August 22, 2024, https://www.britannica.com/topic/messiah-religion.

9   For a further discussion on this topic, see T. D. Alexander's essay "The Messianic Hope," The Gospel Coalition, https://www.thegospelcoalition.org/essay/the-messianic-hope/.

10   Jennifer C. Lane, "Sitting Enthroned: A Scriptural Perspective," *Religious Educator* 19, no. 1 (2018), https://rsc.byu.edu/vol-19-no-1-2018/sitting-enthroned-scriptural-perspective.

11   Scott Volk (with Robert J. Gladstone) makes this claim in his book *Jesus Was Not a Christian* (Burning Ones Publishing, 2019). The book looks at how an insufficient grasp of the Jewishness of Jesus leads to a marginalized view of his mission and calling of the Christian church.

12   Of course, this question only makes sense if we believe those early Scriptures already knew what they were saying. I don't see the Old Testament as a primitive or incomplete revelation waiting to be illuminated, but as the foundation on which everything else stands.

13   Sophiee Suguy, *Judaism Is Not Christianity Minus Jesus*, https://nojesus4jews.weebly.com/.

14   Throughout Scripture, "heaven and earth" functions as a figure of speech referring not to the physical dissolution of the universe but to the passing of the present world order (Isaiah 65:17, Jeremiah 31:35–36, Matthew 24:35). The phrase often serves to contrast the enduring faithfulness of God and his covenant word with the transience of creation. By invoking this language, Jesus heightens—not diminishes—the Torah's permanence: even if the cosmos were to fade, the divine word that created and sustains it would remain.

15   Deanna A. Thompson, *Deuteronomy* (Westminster John Knox Press, 2014), 12.

16   Later Christian theology interpreted these realities through the cross and resurrection, identifying Jesus as the true temple, the eternal priest, and the perfect sacrifice. My argument here concerns the prophetic vision that Jesus affirmed, not the later ecclesial developments that grew from it.

17   Don Finto, *Your People Shall Be My People: How Israel, the Jews, and the Christian Church Will Come Together in the Last Days* (Chosen Books, 2001). Finto paints a Jewish picture of the first believers throughout his work.

18   Most scholars agree that this term was coined by outsiders to describe a Jewish movement that had begun to include non-Jews. At this point in history it was a sociological label, rather than a theological break. Others have also said it referred to a group of Jews who followed Jesus's "way." See F. F. Bruce, *The Book of Acts* (Eerdmans, 1988), 231; Everett Ferguson, *Backgrounds of Early Christianity*, 3rd ed. (Eerdmans, 2003).

19   Yonatan Adler, "The First Synagogues," Biblical Archaeology Society, https://library.biblicalarchaeology.org/sidebar/the-first-synagogues/. This article explores the emergence of early synagogues in the first century CE, highlighting their role as educational institutions rather than places of worship. He emphasizes that these synagogues facilitated the public reading and interpretation of the Torah, serving as a primary means for disseminating its laws among ordinary Judeans, particularly during the Hasmonean period.

20   Charles A. Sullivan, "Church, Synagogue, and Paul," January 31, 2019, https://charlesasullivan.com/12848/church-synagogue-st-paul/. Sullivan describes early Messianic gatherings as "para-synagogue organizations woven deeply into the fabric of first-century Judaism," emphasizing that their structure remained distinctly Jewish.

21   Gentile "sympathizers," mentioned by Philo (*On the Virtues* 102) and Josephus (*Ant.* 14.110, *War* 2.454), closely parallel descriptions of God-fearers; they adopted Jewish ethical monotheism without being full proselytes. See Louis H. Feldman, "The Omnipresence of the God-Fearers," *Biblical Archaeology Review* 12, no. 5 (1986): 58–63; see also Shaye J. D. Cohen, *From the Maccabees to the Mishnah* (Westminster Press, 1987), 57–59.

22   The Old Testament also recognizes these groups, though converts are usually called "sojourners" who joined themselves to Israel.

23   The writings of several early Church fathers illustrate a deepening hostility toward Jewish tradition and identity. The *Epistle of Barnabas* (late 1st–early 2nd century) interprets Israel's covenant as void and claims that Christians are the true heirs of God's promises (Barn. 4:6–7; 13:1). Justin Martyr's *Dialogue with Trypho* (ca. 155 CE) depicts his Jewish conversation partner as stubbornly blind to Christ's revelation and later develops the idea that the Jews suffer justly as those rejected by God. Ignatius of Antioch warns Gentile believers not to "live according to Judaism" (*Magnesians* 10). Melito of Sardis's *Peri Pascha* (ca. 170 CE) presents Israel as complicit in the death of God—a theme later expanded by Hippolytus of Rome in his *Expository Treatise against the Jews*. By the time of Constantine, this antagonism had become codified in law: Jews were barred from living in Jerusalem and forbidden, under penalty of death by burning, from dissuading converts to Christianity. The Council of Nicaea (325 CE) sealed the divide, decreeing that the

Church's observance of Easter must not coincide with "the custom of the Jews," thereby institutionalizing the separation between Christianity and its Jewish roots. See also Joel Richardson, *When a Jew Rules the World* (WND Books, 2015).

24   James Carroll, *Constantine's Sword: The Church and the Jews* (Houghton Mifflin, 2001), 145.

25   Pamela Eisenbaum's *Paul Was Not a Christian* (HarperOne, 2009) offers a compelling study of Paul's life and writings, showing his faith and mission remained firmly rooted in Pharisaic Judaism. The same logic, I believe, extends to the apostles and the first generation of believers.

26   The formal separation—marked by new liturgies and the development of the Mass—slowly evolved over several generations. At this point, we're speaking of the very earliest, literal disciples of Jesus, whose worship remained entirely within Jewish life, as recorded by Acts.

27   In his comprehensive study *The Partings of the Ways*, 2nd ed. (SCM Press, 2006), James D. G. Dunn argues that the first believers described in the New Testament still understood themselves as fully Jewish. Though their confession of Jesus as Messiah set them apart as a distinctive group within Judaism, their faith and practice remained well within the boundaries of Second Temple and Hellenistic Jewish life.

28   James Carrol (among others) asserts that the first believers celebrated Eucharist as the Passover meal for at least the first few decades of the Jesus movement. See *Constantine's Sword,* 145.

29   While scholarly opinions vary on the precise form of bread and cup practice in the New Testament era, the formal liturgy—later known as the Eucharist and eventually formalized into the Mass—did not exist in the apostolic period. Early believers met for prayer, teaching, and shared meals within the framework of synagogue and Jewish life (Acts 2:42–46, 1 Corinthians 11), though in some communities these gatherings reflected elements of the surrounding Greco-Roman banquet culture. Since the apostolic communities were founded mostly by Jews, and the Council of Jerusalem's concern centered on preserving table fellowship between Jew and Gentile, it is reasonable to conclude that the bread and cup remained rooted in Jewish meal tradition at this time. Descriptions of more structured Eucharistic worship appear by the mid-second century (e.g., Justin

Martyr, *First Apology* 66–67), but liturgy was not standardized until the fourth century, following Constantine's legalization of Christianity (313 CE) and the organizational developments that followed the Council of Nicaea (325 CE).

30   Jewish scholar Pamela Eisenbaum argues that Paul never ceased to identify as Jewish and should be understood as a figure within Judaism, not outside it. She portrays him as a devout, Greek-speaking Pharisaic Jew whose belief in Jesus as Messiah expanded, rather than replaced, his Jewish worldview. According to Eisenbaum, Paul's mission to the Gentiles was not an attempt to found a new religion but to invite non-Jews into a right relationship with Israel's God through the promises made to Abraham. Her work challenges the traditional Christian portrait of Paul as the founder of Christianity and supports the view that his theology and practice remained firmly rooted in the covenantal framework of Second Temple Judaism. See her book, *Paul Was Not a Christian* (HarperOne, 2009).

31   E. Randolph Richards and Richard James, *Misreading Scripture with Individualist Eyes: Patronage, Honor, and Shame in the Biblical World* (IVP Academic, 2020).

32   In Acts, "the Way" is the earliest self-identifier for the Jesus movement, highlighting its inclusion within Judaism rather than a formal new religion. See Acts 9:2 and 24:14,22.

33   D. Thomas Lancaster, *Galatians: Sermons from a Messianic Perspective* (First Fruits of Zion, 2011), offers a Messianic Jewish reading of Paul's letter, emphasizing Torah observance and Gentile inclusion in God's covenant.

34   Ibid., 89–96. This perspective suggests that Paul's opposition to "works of the law" was not a rejection of the Torah itself but a critique of the belief that Gentiles must adopt these specific Jewish identity markers to be justified before God.

35   The Sabbath (Shabbat) functioned as a covenant sign uniquely given to Israel (Exodus 31:16–17, Ezekiel 20:12), yet it was also extended to "the sojourner within your gates" (Exodus 20:10, Deuteronomy 5:14). Later, Isaiah 56:6–7 reaffirms this inclusion, blessing the foreigners who "join themselves to the Lord" and "keep the Sabbath." Gentiles who attached themselves to Israel's God were therefore invited into Sabbath rest, even if they were not bound by the detailed rabbinic traditions that developed later. In the first century, Gentile believers who worshiped alongside

Jews in synagogues naturally participated in Sabbath gatherings (Acts 13:42–44). The apostles never imposed Sabbath observance as a Gentile requirement, yet they also prohibited anyone from judging another regarding such matters (Romans 14:5–6, Colossians 2:16). This pattern reflects continuity with Torah's vision for Sabbath among Gentiles rather than its abolition—Gentiles were welcomed into Israel's worship life while remaining distinctly Gentile.

36   N. T. Wright, *Justification: God's Plan and Paul's Vision* (IntraVarsity Press, 2009), 116–17. Wright suggests that "works of the law" in Paul's context refers to the things that assured a person's status in belonging to God's covenant people, not the moral "good works" questioned by the Reformed tradition.

37   This interpretation aligns with what many modern scholars call the "New Perspective on Paul," which argues that Paul's concern was not with Torah obedience as such, but with how Torah functioned as a boundary between Jews and Gentiles. More recent scholarship, often termed the "Paul Within Judaism" approach (e.g., Mark D. Nanos; Magnus Zetterholm), sharpens this further, arguing that Paul remained fully within Judaism and addressed the question of how Gentiles could be incorporated into Israel's covenant without becoming Jews. Other scholars, however, continue to interpret the phrase more broadly, as referring to human efforts at righteousness apart from divine grace. I find the former line of interpretation more persuasive. The so-called "New Perspective" recovers Paul's own historically rooted viewpoint, while the "Paul Within Judaism" approach carries that recovery to its most coherent conclusion.

38   "One Law and the Gentiles," FirstFruits of Zion Torah Portions, https://ffoz. org/torahportions/commentary/one-law-and-the-gentiles.

39   "The Background and Purpose of Hebrews," Third Mill, https://thirdmill.org/ seminary/lesson.asp/vid/181.

40   James Rochford, "Hebrews," Evidence Unseen, https://evidenceunseen.com/ new-testament/hebrews.

41   "The Death of James the Just," Christian History for the Everyman, https:// www.christian-history.org/death-of-james.html.

42   Most Christian traditions interpret Christ's sacrifice as rendering the temple system obsolete. I challenge that reading, particularly in relation to Hebrews. The New Testament nowhere depicts the first believers abandoning temple

worship or establishing alternative rituals in its place. The substantial scholarship cited throughout these notes makes it difficult to dismiss. To read Hebrews sympathetically within its first-century context, we must avoid imposing later Christian constructs onto an audience that had not yet adopted them.

43   The author and audience of Hebrews were steeped in Jewish apocalyptic eschatology—a worldview anticipating God's visible reign on earth, the resurrection of the dead, and the renewal of creation. Texts such as *1 Enoch, 4 Ezra*, along with the Hebrew Bible, shaped this imagination. Jesus taught the same hope of resurrection and kingdom renewal (Matthew 19:28, 24:29–31; Luke 22:29–30), and the New Testament continues it. Revelation, Jude, and 2 Peter assume it, and Hebrews calls it an "elementary principle" (Hebrews 6:1–2). Paul taught it to Gentile believers in Thessalonica (1 Thessalonians 4:13–18, 2 Thessalonians 1:5–10). This hope was standard among the first followers of Jesus.

44   D. Thomas Lancaster, *The Holy Epistle to the Hebrews: Sermons on a Messianic Jewish Approach,* vol. 1 (Fruitfruits of Zion, 2024). Lancaster challenges the supersessionist reading of Hebrews, offering a messianic perspective on the text.

45   Travis M. Snow, *The Biblical Feasts and the Return of Jesus* (Shiloh Media, 2023), 192.

46   This final accomplishment comes when God finally takes the sin away entirely from Israel, linked to the Messiah's return. See Romans 11:27.

47   Jeff Myers, *Should Christians Support Israel?* (Summit Ministries, 2024), 15.

48   "Statement of Principles," The Temple Institute, https://templeinstitute.org/statement-of-principles-2/

49   Ibid.

50   "Frequently Asked Questions," The Temple Institute, https://templeinstitute.org/frequently-asked-questions/.

51   Matt Davis, host, *The Jewish Road Podcast*, season 8, episode 146, "Still Chosen: Why Are So Many Christians Confused About Israel Right Now?," September 12, 2025.

52   Jeff Myers asks whether Christians should support Israel in light of the October 7, 2024, attacks and provides a guide for seeking a biblical worldview in an impossible situation in his *Should Christians Support Israel?*

53   See https://www.gatherthenations.org/.